THEDA♥CARE
CENTER FOR
HEALTHCARE VALUE

*Targeting Value, Spreading Change*

Other titles available from

THEDA♡CARE
CENTER FOR
HEALTHCARE VALUE

*On the Mend: Revolutionizing Healthcare*
*to Save Lives and Transform the Industry*

by John Toussaint, MD
and Roger A. Gerard, PhD

*Potent Medicine:*
*The Collaborative Cure for Healthcare*

by John Toussaint, MD
with Emily Adams

# Beyond Heroes:
# A Lean Management System
# for Healthcare

by Kim Barnas

with Emily Adams

Forewords by Jim Womack and John Toussaint, MD

THEDACARE
CENTER FOR
HEALTHCARE VALUE
Appleton, WI

THEDACARE
CENTER FOR
HEALTHCARE VALUE

*Targeting Value, Spreading Change*

ThedaCare Center for Healthcare Value
100 W. Lawrence Street
Appleton, WI 54911 USA
createvalue.org

Publisher's Cataloging-in-Publication Data
Barnas, Kim.

    Beyond heroes : a lean management system for healthcare / by Kim Barnas with Emily Adams ; forewords by John Toussaint and Jim Womack. – Appleton, WI : ThedaCare Center for Healthcare Value, 2014.

    p. ; cm.

    ISBN13: 978-0-9848848-2-7

    1. Health services administration. 2. Medical care--United States--Management. 3. Hospitals--United States--Administration. 4. Leadership. 5. Lean manufacturing. 6. ThedaCare (Wisconsin) I. Title. II. Adams, Emily.

    RA971.B37 2014
    362.1068—dc23     2014931331

FIRST EDITION

Project coordination by Jenkins Group, Inc.
BookPublishing.com

*Interior layout by Brooke Camfield*

Printed in the United States of America

18  17  16  15  14  •  5  4  3  2  1

FSC
www.fsc.org
MIX
Paper from
responsible sources
FSC® C002589

This book is dedicated to the people of ThedaCare who shared this journey and offered their energy, intelligence, and courage in the pursuit of better healthcare.

To download the graphics from *Beyond Heroes*,
visit createvalue.org/beyondheroes
Type in the passcode: TrueNorth

# Contents

# Foreword

I f the history of revolution around the globe has taught us one thing, it is this: leadership succeeds only when it learns to evolve. No matter how necessary and just the rebellion, when the dust clears, the leaders need to govern, to make systems work in order to keep a country or an organization running. And that requires an ongoing willingness to change and adapt.

For nearly a decade, the lean revolution in healthcare centered on improving quality and reducing costs in advance of the huge systemic changes we all knew were coming. With healthcare bills bankrupting families and threatening to do the same to the United States, major hospitals and health-system leaders began experimenting with various improvement methods. A healthy percentage of those organizations embraced lean thinking and adopted tools and methods from the Toyota Production System.

Many of us who saw the results of lean thinking in healthcare became true believers. We used the tools to halve the amount of time it took to deliver a life-saving balloon angioplasty to a heart attack victim.

We removed wasted time, movement, and resources from clinical processes and achieved better results with lower costs. Patients were happier; frontline staff were more engaged and energized. We wrote books and gave talks about our successes. The scientific method as interpreted by car manufacturers was going to save the American healthcare system.

And then it seemed like everyone hit a wall.

That statement may sound overly broad, but I have toured, investigated, and advised more than a hundred healthcare organizations in a dozen countries in recent years and have seen the impact. Cross-functional teams of nurses, physicians, pharmacists, and administrators made amazing, weekly breakthroughs in better patient care processes and then watched in dismay as the old ways crept back in and took over. Executives who eagerly supported lean thinking kept looking for the promised resource savings to hit the bottom line and wondered what went wrong. For many, it seemed like value-stream mapping and kaizen improvement projects were just tricks pulled from a shallow bag. Enthusiasm for the hard work of a lean transformation waned in some quarters.

It turns out that revolutionary change is necessary, but it is not sufficient.

The kinds of change that come from rapid process improvements are essential but are only the first steps of a lean journey. The core work of the transformation is changing the culture—changing how we respond to problems, how we think about patients, how we interact with each other. This is an issue not only in healthcare organizations; we have also seen manufacturing, service companies, retailers, and government agencies all struggle with the same issues. When lean thinking goes only skin deep and management does not change, improvements cannot be sustained, and savings never quite hit the bottom line.

Knowing this, I have watched with great interest as Kim Barnas and her team at ThedaCare hospitals in Wisconsin worked at transforming their culture by redesigning the system of daily management. After two years of experimentation, discussion, and study, they found a more deliberative approach to leading a lean healthcare system. By changing the expectations of what managers and frontline supervisors actually do each day, Kim and her team pushed the roots of lean deeper into the organization. This encouraged new ways of thinking, which led to new behaviors. Instead of adding continuous improvement to the list of manager's duties, improvement became the organizing principle of their work. Thus, a new management system emerged and it was clear that this was the secret sauce that so many had been seeking.

Kim discovered that changing a leader's work content changed the leader as well. From frontline supervisors to top executives, new management duties encouraged everyone to become more respectful, improvement focused, and process orientated. Instead of managing by exception—running after today's unique emergency—they fixed processes. They standardized processes. In doing so, more improvements to clinical processes remained in place. Projects initiated by frontline caregivers were aligned with the hospital's major initiatives *and* relevant to the unit or clinic. Continuous improvement became the working method instead of the extra task.

And finally, dozens of managers in ThedaCare's two major hospitals knew exactly what they were supposed to do and had the time to do it. In the first six years of ThedaCare's lean revolution, we lost many area managers. Some of that turnover would have occurred anyway, as always happens in periods of great change, but the enormity of that shift was a clear sign that managers were under too much pressure. Since 2010, when the business performance system began creating a supportive structure for leaders, just two area managers have left.

Next, Kim and her team started teaching their *business performance system* to other hospitals that were struggling to make improvements stick, from Canada to California. The system not only translates to other organizations, it usually thrives.

Let's be clear: ThedaCare's experiments and methods are not perfect. They will benefit from continuous improvement and every organization will need to customize the system to fit its needs. Still, we believe that this business performance system is a breakthrough in thinking about leadership.

We are finally moving beyond the age of heroes chasing exceptions and are looking forward to innovations in management that will move us even further ahead. The faster we can implement these ideas, the better it will be for all of us—patients, physicians, nurses, managers, and everyone who pays for healthcare.

—John Toussaint, MD
Founder and CEO, ThedaCare Center for Healthcare Value
January 2014

## An Additional Word to Those Readers from Outside Healthcare

Why should managers and process improvers from other industries consult a book on lean healthcare management? Based on personal experience—as patients or as family members of a patient—many outsiders will surely think the term "healthcare management" is an oxymoron. And, until recently, that view was quite right. But times have changed, and in these pages readers from other industries will find a dramatic story of how the management team at ThedaCare conducted a series of experiments to pioneer a new way of managing that is relevant to any organization in any industry.

The ThedaCare team built on a solid foundation of rigorous process improvement with an equally rigorous process of policy deployment (*hoshin kanri*) to determine and communicate the organization's True North goals. Many readers from other industries will have done the same. But then the ThedaCare team pioneered a daily lean management system (which they call their business performance system) for every manager from the frontline supervisor to the president. And this breakthrough is what every organization in every industry needs now.

What are the principles of a lean management system?

Managing by process, using A3 and plan-do-study-adjust (PDSA) analysis, rather than the traditional method of managing by exception—the firefighting of things gone wrong that occupied most of the manager's time—and managing by metrics set up by senior managers (which occupied the rest of the manager's time).

Managing by using the "Five Whys" to identify the root cause of problems rather than assigning blame to one person.

Managing patient pathways end-to-end within product families of diagnosis and treatment rather than optimizing individual points along these journeys.

Finally, problem solving and improvement by line managers and their teams, with technical assistance from the staff "lean team," rather than the reverse, which is still the norm in most organizations.

And, what are the methods of a lean management system? ThedaCare uses the annual True North exercise to prioritize the key challenges and opportunities for the organization and to cascade these priorities down to every level for action. (This is separate from the familiar annual budget cycle, which is still needed but in the background rather than the foreground.) Many organizations have already done this but without obtaining the hoped-for results because of the weakness in line management and instability throughout their enterprise.

ThedaCare employs an A3-based PDSA process. This is not just for attacking problems at every level (e.g., excessive patient time between the emergency department and reaching a bed in a unit) but also for seizing opportunities (e.g., achieving an industry-leading reduction in drug reconciliation errors). Again, many organizations have embraced these methods but without the expected results due to weak deployment on the front lines.

They use standard work for all value-creating and incidental work in the enterprise—designed, documented, and continually audited, revised, and improved by line managers and work teams. This is the heart of the matter. Without creating stability in every work activity by means of standard work, sustainable improvement will continue to be elusive.

They also use daily standard work for every manager at every level, up to and including the president of the ThedaCare hospitals. This is the secret behind sustainable standard work: Daily observation of the work at each level by line management, with periodic improvement of the work.

Is this management process easy? Definitely not. Can it be introduced without the direct, hands-on participation of senior management? Absolutely not. And is it perfect? Definitely, absolutely not. The author insists that what they have achieved so far only lays the groundwork for continuous improvement of their management system. For example, the challenge of managing the patient's journey end-to-end—across primary care, hospital care, and then continuing maintenance through the life cycle, often flowing through independent organizations—still lies ahead.

This said, I now find myself in an unexpected position. I am recommending this book to managers in other industries far removed from healthcare who have had some success with lean tools but who have struggled to create a management system that can fully utilize these tools on a continuing basis. I do this with the realization that ThedaCare is now far ahead of most organizations I visit in other industries in deploying lean management, even though these other companies started their lean journeys years earlier. This is an amazing turn of events, given the state of healthcare management only a few years ago, and one that gives me hope for lean management in every industry: If the managers at ThedaCare could progressively create a lean management system through several years of experiments—a system that eliminates the need for management heroics to put out ever-burning fires—and do this in an industry with perhaps the worst management practices, managers in other industries now have no excuse for failing to follow their example.

However, let me be clear that I am not advocating painting by the numbers. No reader from other industries can or should literally copy what ThedaCare has done. (And ThedaCare's best practices for lean management will continue to evolve in any case.) But readers from every industry can and should learn from ThedaCare's story and then set off on a journey of exploration to create a lean management system suited to their circumstances. I hope you will be one of those readers.

—Jim Womack
Founder and Senior Advisor, Lean Enterprise Institute
January 2014

*Success is not final, failure is not fatal:*
*it is the courage to continue that counts.*

—Winston Churchill

# Chapter 1

# Drowning
## Our Leaders

For me it was the big time. Coming from a small health system in Battle Creek, Michigan, 1994, I had been recruited to create a philanthropic foundation for the large and well-regarded Appleton Medical Center. While being courted by the chairman of the board of trustees and the president of the hospitals, I was told that the future was mine to create.

Excited and proud, I moved my young family 350 miles across the great Lake Michigan to Appleton, Wisconsin and showed up for my first day of work. The hospital president took me to meet my secretary in her office. Then he showed me to my office, swinging open the door to reveal a large, empty space with a telephone sitting forlornly in the middle of the room. When I turned around, he was grinning.

"You're going to build this foundation from the bottom up," he said. "To do that you need to learn how to navigate our system. So here's the bottom: you find your own office furniture and supplies. Use your secretary and use the phone book to figure out how to get the things you need."

This was the old, time-tested leadership training program known as *throw her in the deep end.* Perhaps you have gone through this so-called training and know the feeling of seeing your peers step back and watch to see whether you can swim. It builds character, right?

Of course, the problem with sink-or-swim training is that some perfectly good puppies drown. If not aligned with the organization's vision, a new manager or executive can quickly fall off course, wasting valuable time and resources and damaging reputations as they flail. And yet, this is how leaders are generally welcomed into new positions: without training or a map to guide them, we leave them to their own devices. It is our first strike against new leaders.

Luckily, I did not flail in Appleton. As the two-hospital system grew to include five hospitals, 22 clinics, nursing homes, and rehabilitation centers unified under the name ThedaCare, my role grew steadily as well. I created another philanthropic foundation to benefit Theda Clark Hospital in Neenah, Wisconsin, and then took on a third for ThedaCare's hospice program. Meanwhile the parent, not-for-profit ThedaCare, became a complete cradle-to-grave health system and is now the largest employer in northeast Wisconsin, serving more than 350,000 patients annually. Since 2003, we have also been working hard to transform ThedaCare into a lean organization.

Lean was a serious initiative from the beginning. It was energetically championed by our CEO at that time, John Toussaint, MD, who began his own lean investigations in 2002. By this time, I was a vice president with operational responsibilities in the hospitals for obstetrics, cancer care, and surgery, in addition to the philanthropic foundations, so I was involved from the beginning of our ambitious lean initiative.

Like many organizations beginning a lean initiative, we started by putting together teams to map our value streams. First, though, we had to define "value stream." In industry, value streams show how products and information flow through a company from raw material to fabrication and shipping. In healthcare, we decided, the patient was the product, and so the value stream would be the flow of a patient through a cycle of care. A cancer value stream, for instance, includes testing, diagnosis, treatment, and, some percentage of the time, hospice. For women having babies, our obstetrics value stream began with prenatal checkups, continued through delivery, and ended with baby's first visit with a pediatrician. In this way, we shifted our focus from organizing work around specialized departments (silos) such as pharmacy or surgery to organizing around the needs of the patient. We recognized that most patients flow through multiple value streams. Also, we learned that our first pass at any patient's care was disease specific— not necessarily taking multiple health issues into account.

Next, we set end-to-end improvement goals in those value streams— cutting through departments and old barriers—and pushed ahead with three or four *kaizen*[1] improvement teams operating every week across the organization. Our Friday report-out sessions were part information sharing, part tent revival. We trained more than two dozen people to become lean experts facilitating kaizen teams and then started rotating frontline leaders and executives through those facilitator positions for two-year terms. Organizing all the work was our ThedaCare Improvement System Office, overseen by a senior vice president reporting to the CEO.

We called our kaizen team weeks Rapid Improvement Events and made sure they were multidisciplinary, with nurses, patients, pharmacy technicians, family members, and doctors all joining together to solve problems. Wherever we applied lean thinking, quality was improving, costs were falling, and patient satisfaction was inching upward.

---

1. "Kaizen" is from the Japanese symbols meaning "change" and "good." It is translated as "change for the better" and usually refers to a lean improvement project in which a cross-functional team studies and then improves an area or process in one week.

Like most of my fellow leaders, I saw the benefits of lean as the economy stagnated in the mid-2000s and cost pressures on healthcare increased. We had all seen plenty of improvement programs, but lean was the first that was a complete operating system, balancing the needs of patients, caregivers, and the bottom line. Lean thinking was helping us improve quality for patients, reduce costs, and engage employees like no other approach.

About three years into this initiative, sometime in 2006, I was involved in improvement events in a cancer treatment value stream focusing on radiation oncology. We were getting breakthrough results: improving labor productivity[2] by 20%, improving same-day access to one's doctor by 30%, and slashing the time it took to move a patient from diagnosis to treatment from weeks to days. After a slow start, physicians had become more engaged in lean and were sometimes driving improvement work. Patients were on every kaizen team, helping to shape and guide our priorities. Sustaining our improved processes was a struggle, but I was sure we would solve that problem, too. It felt like we were sailing with a strong tailwind.

Then we hit a snag that could have sunk our lean initiative. And the snag was us. What hospital executives were asking of our line managers was slowly strangling our lean improvement efforts. We were heaping on more work, expecting managers to guide lean efforts while performing the same managerial duties as before, in the same way as before. And we expected them to figure out *how* on their own. This was nothing new. Like our throw-her-in-the-deep-end training, these competing priorities were another strike against our leaders.

---

2.  At the highest level, productivity at ThedaCare is defined as gross revenue per full-time employee equivalent. At the unit level, managers track worked hours per unit of service to define productivity. A unit of service might be a lab report, a surgery, or 24 hours in a medical-unit bed.

One day, the very frustrated manager of a hospital intensive care unit yelled at me in my office (in a respectful Wisconsin way, of course), "You've changed the way our teams work, but you haven't changed how we lead. We don't have the tools for this."

Another manager wept in my office. Both of these were good and steady leaders, so I knew there was a real problem. I talked to other managers and to executives in ThedaCare's two main hospitals, and everyone recognized the truth of the ICU manager's statement and acknowledged the general frustration. Managers at ThedaCare are dead center—the bull's-eye—of our leadership structure. They are responsible for frontline supervisors and entire units; they answer to vice presidents and other executives. New and daunting responsibilities were pressing down from above and below. It was no wonder that cracks were starting to show at this level.

For nearly two years, we had been telling managers that the most important goal was improving patient experiences by improving the value streams they managed and then sustaining those improvements. But we at the executive levels were still acting as if hitting monthly financial targets in the budget—mostly unrelated to improvement work—was the real objective. Goals were being generated in boardrooms, but these were often inconsistent with what was happening at the front line. Worse yet, we were failing to offer meaningful communication, training, or guidance to the line managers now responsible for keeping all the critical improvement work on track.

We resolved to do something and reached forward to find a solution without quite grasping the extent of the project. It turned out to be enormous, even though our scope was limited to ThedaCare's two largest hospitals and not yet the whole organization. I thought we had a leadership process that just needed some tweaks. I had forgotten that empty office I was given on my first day. Fortunately, other people in

ThedaCare were also investigating ways to improve the way we manage processes and how we train our leaders—from supervisors to managers and executives. We were able to use the expertise of people in our support services, such as human resources and the lean improvement office, as we put together a team and began investigating ways to make—or remake, depending on your perspective—our system of leading and managing.

This book is the story of the experiments we ran, our successes and failures, and the new system we developed. We are offering our story because I know from visits to dozens of hospitals and healthcare organizations that our problem is everyone's problem. Healthcare organizations have embarked on lean programs at a very fast clip, but few see the need to update their leadership or management techniques. As a result, they end up undermining their efforts as quickly as they make operational improvements.

Before we go further, brief definitions of *leadership* and *management* are necessary. Leadership invokes heroism or charisma at the top. Management often sounds like the activities of a functionary in the middle ranks of an organization. Neither definition is useful. I like to say that we manage processes and lead people. The system I will describe in the chapters ahead offers a method for managing the work of leaders, as well as developing and mentoring those leaders. Because this system involves leading and managing, as well as learning to understand the business of a clinic or hospital unit and how it performs in order to drive performance, we called it our business performance system. With this name we remind ourselves every day that improving the performance of the business is the focus of our leaders, just as taking the best possible care of our patients is the work of everyone in our hospitals.

As we begin, it will also be helpful to understand our leadership structure. ThedaCare is a complex organization with six tiers of leadership in the hospitals. (See illustration below.) At the front line are clinical leads who have limited managerial duties on their shift, in their unit. They take care of patients, make sure the shift is fully staffed, ensure their colleagues get adequate breaks, and lead some quality improvement activities. Next are supervisors, who oversee the work of a few clinical leads and are also in direct contact with patients. Supervisors manage the flow of a unit, interface with physicians, help create staffing models, and mentor their clinical leads.

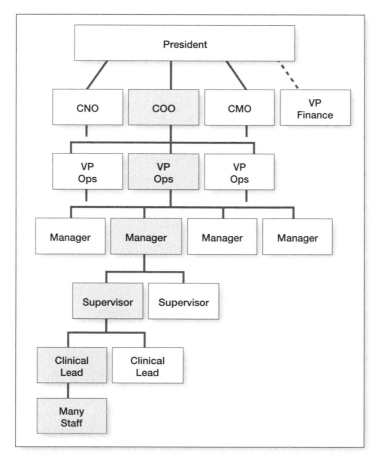

**ThedaCare Leadership Structure Chart**

Direct patient contact is no longer in the equation once we reach the level of managers, who mentor and guide two to four supervisors each and are responsible for the business of a clinic or unit. (Clinics are doctors' offices grouped by specialty, seeing outpatients. Units are for patients admitted to the hospital.) We have 35 managers working in our two major hospitals.

Vice presidents have similar yet broader responsibilities in that they oversee managers and larger areas or value streams. ThedaCare's two main hospitals, Appleton Medical Center and Theda Clark Medical Center, have a total of three VPs who report to the chief operating officer. The COO is a member of the executive level of leadership that includes the chief nursing officer and chief medical officer, who oversee all nurses and physicians, respectively. The three executives report to the president (that's me) at the final leadership level.

The business performance system we have built at ThedaCare, which I think of as the common rudder for steering all of our efforts, involves some radical ideas. We have frontline leaders—from ICU nursing supervisors to clinical leads in radiation—talking to their managers every day about the state of the business. That's right. This not-for-profit healthcare system trains all leaders to think of their units as small businesses entwined in one larger business. We know that if we do not have a healthy business, we will not be around long to care for our patients. ThedaCare executives have always placed high value on our financial stewardship and the public trust. Developing business acumen in all leaders just takes the idea further. We want frontline supervisors, area managers, and executives talking about the health of their businesses. That means tracking unit costs as well as safety issues and patient needs.

We have also created standard work for clinical leads, supervisors, managers, and executives that guides our daily work. Instead of setting our leaders adrift with a long list of goals to be met, we created a framework for gathering information, addressing problems, mentoring new leaders, and guiding improvement work.

For instance, standard work for every manager includes a no-meeting zone from 8 to 10 a.m. every morning. During that time, everyone knows managers will be at *gemba*[3] collecting information from supervisors and clinical leads. Standard work includes the specific questions that managers ask based on the current needs of the unit such as, "What issues affecting patient safety do you foresee today?" The manager can translate that information into new improvement work. Executives also have standard work. For example, a vice president and the chief operating officer meet each Tuesday morning with the manager of surgery, at gemba, to talk about performance and barriers. This is understood as a coaching opportunity as well as information gathering.[4]

Our chief operating officer follows and regularly audits her standard work. As president of the ThedaCare hospitals, I also have standard work. Since all standard work is informed by the organization's True North metrics—which are our few selected enterprise goals in five categories—every leader's standard work is linked to the efforts of every other leader, ensuring that we are all rowing in the same direction. It is just one aspect of our business performance system, but it has been revolutionary. We will explore our True North metrics and how we use them to link all standard work in chapter 3.

All of this has been undertaken in an attempt to replace firefighting with preemptive improvement work. In a hospital environment we are accustomed to firefighting, which is jumping to the quickest solution without really analyzing the problem. When something goes wrong or

---

3. A Japanese word popularized by the Toyota Production System, "gemba" means the place where real value is created. In a hospital, gemba is located wherever caregivers are directly helping patients.

4. Chapter 11 offers a more complete description of standard work at all levels.

real emergencies arise, the person who steps in to fix it with a quick solution is the hero. We like being heroes. But it is a problem to have 6,000 well-meaning heroes tackling problems in 6,000 different ways, often without regard to the needs of upstream, downstream, or parallel processes. Firefighting provides a short-term high but is a long-term drain on everyone's time and resources. What we want instead are carefully considered, deliberate, team-based countermeasures to attack problems. Even better, we want those problems attacked before they materialize as issues. We believe that without the need to be heroes, leaders can systematically address problems and leave no one in the organization adrift to sink or swim.

Four years into our experiment, I can report some remarkable results. In my role as head of the hospitals, I do 80% less firefighting. I complete my daily work faster than I dreamed possible. I work on larger issues such as improving community access to healthcare, improving the way in which we help patients navigate care, and managing to financial targets rather than getting sucked into a constant stream of emergencies. Supervisors and managers report greater confidence in their teams and increased job satisfaction since adopting standard work.

"Some people might think my job sounds repetitive, doing the same thing, asking the same questions of my team every day," says Vicki Van Epps, a supervisor in our radiation oncology unit. "But for me, the structure means there's no guessing. I know what I'm doing now and where I can find capacity to do anything extra."

The story of how we got here is important because, in creating a business performance system, the process is just as important as the product. A common Toyota saying is, "If the process is right, the product [the results] will be right." Keep that in mind. Healthcare is filled with highly educated people working in an often-emotional environment, and respect is essential when developing a new business performance system.

This means listening to your people, incorporating their ideas and concerns, running experiments, accepting that some of those experiments will fail, and trying again.

In developing our new system, I often sought the advice of my sensei,[5] Jose Bustillo, who helped me select a team, set an agenda, and rethink all of our assumptions. Following our A3 problem-solving template, the team developed a problem statement that began: "Every manager at ThedaCare manages his or her own way. There is no one system."

Then we created a cause-and-effect diagram, searched for the meaning of good leadership, used the scientific method to design experiments, and set up experimental development labs to keep the scale of our inevitable test failures small. Our process was not always pretty, but I know that if I had dreamed up a perfect plan in isolation and foisted it onto my subordinates, it never would have taken root. I will provide a complete description of our transformational process in the next chapter.

Our goal was a new leadership system in which frontline supervisors, area managers, and upper-level executives all know today's goals, yesterday's performance, and how to work through problems. Within three months, we pulled together a larger team and began writing standard work for supervisors and managers. Our new goal statement was "to develop people, to solve problems, and to improve performance."

Here, in a short story, is how our lives have changed four years later. Let's say that in the years before our business performance system, the hospital suffered a financial setback and the president—busy fighting fires—ordered a 3% cost reduction across the board. The team of nurses and technicians working in the intensive care unit threw up their hands and said, "There's nothing we can cut. We're already understaffed and spend all day on the run, caring for our patients."

---

5. *Sensei* usually refers to a teacher with advanced lean knowledge and experience.

Their supervisor, valiantly protecting her people, also protested under-staffing, and the problem trickled up to the area manager. Aware that the ICU doctors were already grumpy about the nursing staff being thin, the manager made a decision. She cut the staff-training budget to near zero; reduced the hours of the senior, most highly paid, nurses; and created a very disgruntled ICU. One problem was solved, but a worse one was created. Sound familiar?

Here is how that 3% cost reduction issue plays out now. The manager asks the supervisor and her team to start coming up with ideas to reduce costs in the ICU. They are, after all, the frontline experts. In their daily huddles—brief, structured team meetings—the team throws around some ideas and then uses lean tools to see opportunities. They relocate medical supplies and reorganize their drug delivery system. This reduces time spent running around searching for materials. Now, team members can spend more time at the patient bedside and are able to eliminate both overtime and the additional nursing aides who were supplying temporary help during peak hours when it felt like everyone was running ragged. Cost reductions come with greater staff satisfaction and better patient care. I make this sound easy. It is not. It is hard work, but the outcomes are more satisfying and sustainable.

Another critical component of our work has been defining the role of doctors in improvement. Through trial and error over the past decade, we have come to the general rule that physicians are involved in Rapid Improvement Events when we are looking for breakthrough changes in the therapeutic process. If we need to slash the time it takes for a heart attack patient to get from the hospital's front door to a life-saving balloon angioplasty, for instance, we absolutely include doctors on the team because we are planning to improve their work. We also ask for physician input when the issue at hand concerns them, such as unit staffing. Most of the time, however, our daily continuous process improvements do not affect physician treatment paths, so we focus on making changes around the doctor. It is important to note that we do not implement work that affects our physicians without their input and support. If we are going to change the flow of their work, they must be involved. Physicians have an important and ongoing voice in our business performance system. As we look ahead to the enormous changes facing healthcare organizations, we will be relying on the structure we have created to help us—administrators and physicians—adjust to new realities together. We explore this more fully in chapter 12.

Our world here in the upper middle reaches of the country may not be exactly like yours. Maybe our culture looks more like Toronto than Texas. We value a sense of belonging and are suspicious of lone-wolf characters or those who would push themselves forward into a spotlight. In fact, I would like to make it clear that every "I" in this book has a dozen authors, and I am merely the one telling the story on behalf of the hundreds who made it happen.

Every business performance system will be a little different because each must show the fingerprints of the people in that organization and the local culture. There are no shortcuts for creating one. There are, however, a few core concepts that cannot be skipped.

- Every leader begins each day assessing and understanding the status of the business, to see and anticipate issues.

- Problems get solved when teams work methodically through the scientific process.

- The leader is the team; the team is the leader. Although an individual may take the role of team leader, his or her function is to keep the team on track and document the work. On every unit, the true leader is the frontline problem-solving team. Supervisors and managers support those teams.

These core concepts thoughtfully implemented will be a catalyst. Once teams are engaged to solve problems—or to spot issues before they become problems—everyone will spend less time firefighting and more time doing the real work of the enterprise. Leaders will be invigorated to take on new, more global, issues. Change for the better accelerates while sustaining the improvements of a lean system becomes embedded into the DNA of the organization.

We need these changes in healthcare just as we need them in every organization seeking lasting change. So, let's dive into the process of change.

# Chapter 2

# **Finding** Value in a
## (Reverse) Fishbone

K aren Flom knew she was losing her audience. That morning, just like every other, she gathered a team from her radiation oncology unit around the big board of metrics to discuss *the numbers*. As manager, it was her job to keep everyone focused on improvement. So she talked through the charts and watched her team members try to act interested. Everyone was perfectly polite. That was the problem.

It was a young radiation therapist named Hilarie, in her first job out of college, who broke the spell. Hilarie stepped forward and gestured at Karen's carefully constructed wall of data and said, "This has no value to me."

There was a breathless pause, and little jolt of electricity went through the air, like the moment before a tornado arrives, while everyone waited for Karen's reaction. Karen smiled.

"I was actually excited when Hilarie said that," Karen told me later. "I was starting to suspect that people were bored. We were meeting every morning at a board where the numbers were updated only monthly. We weren't making anything better as a result of looking at those numbers. Hilarie was only saying out loud what we all knew.

"I said, 'OK, what can we talk about that will matter to you?' That's when we started identifying the data we really needed."

In seminars and speeches, I return often to this moment from the spring of 2009 as an illustration of an organization on the cusp of a necessary cultural shift. Without being entirely aware of it, we were crossing a bright line. On one side was the old ThedaCare: a top-down organization where the boss was largely unquestioned. Of course, as an organization striving to be lean, we took care to ask nurses and therapists for their opinions, expertise, and suggestions. But telling a boss that her meeting held no value was not within our cultural norm. On the other side of that bright line—the future where we are heading—is an organization in which everyone knows that data-driven improvement is more important than hierarchy and that we strive for better processes in order to aid frontline workers such as Hilarie.

The fact that Hilarie could speak that truth and Karen could hear her and respond the way she did was a profound moment on an average morning, and it marks one of our beginning points as we moved toward a better business performance system.

Up until 2008, our system for solving problems and making decisions used to be like every other hospital's. When there was a problem on the floor, it got tossed to the clinic lead or supervisor to solve. If the supervisor could not fix it, he threw it over the wall to his manager. If the manager could not fix it, she threw it over to her vice president and so on. This last toss happened rarely, as managers usually felt it was a failure to send problems further up the chain. Decisions, on the other hand, began higher up and trickled down.

Even when we were trying very hard to be lean and all of us agreed that the most important work was taking place at the gemba, such as in surgery or an inpatient unit, we executives would still meet in executive offices far from any gemba to talk about priorities, make decisions about resource uses, and push those pronouncements down the chain.

So let's say there were problems on the floor every day relating to needle sticks. Every day, at least one frontline worker was getting injured on the job with a syringe. Individually, each of those incidents would be reported upward to managers. Meanwhile, executives might decide to address employee safety with a new initiative to prevent back injuries because they did not know that needle sticks had become rampant. Coming from two different ends of the leadership chain, the problem and the decision were like two ships passing in the night.

Managers were caught in the middle. Added to the usual stresses of the old leadership system—in which managers were supposed to fix problems at the front lines while hewing to the orders of executives—our managers were now responsible for making sure that we maintained the gains from all those lean improvement projects. That was extra work for which they had no allotted time. And that is what led to the breakdown in my office.

The only thing surprising to me now about MaryJeanne Schaffmeyer's tears in my office that day in 2006 is that they did not come sooner. Now COO of the hospitals, back then MaryJeanne was manager of OB/GYN, which included the very busy and emotionally charged Family Birth Centers in two hospitals. (I was a system vice president at the time.) MaryJeanne had her hands full. A native New Yorker with a gift for storytelling and charismatic leadership, MaryJeanne had embraced the lean transformation. She supported teams that overhauled the patient journey through labor and delivery and reduced the number of babies that required neonatal ICU visits. She was committed to the lean process.

But that day, she felt inadequate. Through tears, she said she feared for her job. "None of the improvements are moving fast enough," she said. "There's so much more I need to know. I don't understand productivity or revenue. Suddenly, I'm expected to understand financial metrics, not just cost management. It's like trying to put new wine in old skins. I'm bursting."

I hugged MaryJeanne and made a promise. I said, "We're going to figure this out, and you're going to help me."

Not long after that, the manager of the intensive care unit came in for a private chat. But she was not crying. She was angry. "How am I supposed to manage in this new world?" she demanded. "I don't know what you expect of me. I don't know how to lead people through this, and that's just disrespectful of my team. All I know is that I am failing, and I have never failed before."

First, I consulted with leadership in ThedaCare's lean improvement office, looking to alleviate the pressure on managers. After talking through the issues, the solution did seem simple. If managers were having a hard time incorporating lean work into their regular work, we should offer lean experts to support them. So, in our first experiment, we came up with a plan that resembled a traveling judge in the old west. We tapped a few experienced facilitators from our lean improvement office and assigned each one to work full-time with a manager for a month or so. These lean experts would help the manager integrate lean activities into his or her daily responsibilities, follow up on improvement projects, and make sure standard work was updated and followed. Then, like a judge who oversaw the legal needs of several small towns, the facilitator would pack up and move on to the next manager who needed help.

The plan worked well while the traveling judge was present. But as soon as the facilitator left for a new area, most managers were again overwhelmed by the amount of "regular" plus "lean" work. Lean work was deprioritized as new fires broke out in their units. The team admitted that the experiment had failed and met to decide on our next move. It is embarrassing to admit, but we opted to try a traveling judge again. Again, it failed as a long-term solution. In all, those early experiments took nearly two years.

So, we circled the wagons and called on the expertise of my lean sensei. Jose Bustillo, a consultant, who had been meeting with me once or twice a month for more than a year so that he could teach me about lean thinking while I taught him about healthcare. After hearing of my struggling managers, he talked to me about the management systems employed by mature lean companies such as automotive airbag maker Autoliv. He described a system in which there was only one way to manage processes, where lean and regular management duties were the same. He urged me to read David Mann's book, *Creating a Lean Culture*.[6] When Mann wrote about traditional managers in industry who were accustomed to "doing whatever it takes" to meet the day's schedule or the month's numbers, and how this attitude undermined a lean transformation, it was easy to recognize our own firefighting tendencies.

On Jose's advice, we started over and put together a steering committee to guide our leadership work. For anyone creating a new system of leadership in an established company, the membership of this initial team will be crucial. Boats will be rocked. There will be misstarts and failures, Jose warned me. The team needed to trust one another in order to weather the failures.

Another good piece of advice: keep both the steering group and the initial project area small, allowing the team to back up and reconfigure when necessary. I am still thankful that I took this advice.

---

6. David Mann, *Creating a Lean Culture: Tools to Sustain Lean Conversions*, CRC Press (2010).

Then it was time to back up and think more broadly about leadership and lean. Jose focused on our use of data, pointing out that updating our metrics monthly meant we were frequently trying to address issues that happened weeks earlier. We were like detectives who let every case grow cold before investigating. Jose drew us diagrams of how manufacturing companies used data. On the shop floor, leaders and workers received fresh performance information on the hour or even in real time. We protested. There was no way our organization could produce relevant data on demand. It was asking too much. Jose pointed out that we were already collecting real-time data during rapid improvement events. We just lacked experience in pulling and using data for daily management.

Jose's proposals looked like nothing I recognized, even after two decades in healthcare leadership. So, instead of plowing ahead, we pulled together a one-week team event that included lean facilitators, managers, another VP, and two outside sensei, and we constructed a reverse-fishbone diagram to begin answering the question: What does good leadership look like in a lean environment? All week we used the fishbone, sometimes called a cause-and-effect diagram, to drill down into what we needed of our leaders and how to get there.[7]

The head of the fish—the final effect of all the causes—we defined in a single statement: leaders will have a framework to simply and easily manage their businesses, develop people, solve problems, and improve performance.

The ribs of the fish, or the causes to create the effect, included statements about driving performance improvement, aligning with strategic deployment, and creating standard work. To make it happen, we agreed that managers would need standard work, visual-defect boards, and reliance on root-cause analysis and other lean tools. In the end, we had

---

7.    The full reverse-fishbone diagram is in the appendix, figure 1.

57 elements of good lean leadership, and our managers in the room were looking nervous. If their workdays felt like wrestling an octopus before, what would work look like in this new world?

That meeting happened in May 2008. Three months later, in August, we reconvened with an expanded team that included more managers for a two-week improvement event in which we developed our first A3.

This description of a problem, goal, gap analysis, countermeasures, and results on a single sheet of standard A3 paper is a central tool at ThedaCare.[8] For this A3, our goal statement was "to develop people, to solve problems, and to improve performance."

The August 2008 team included help from lean facilitators and human resources personnel, which were very important voices in this process. In hospitals, there is often tension between operations—the front line of caregiving—and support functions such as HR or a lean improvement office. If we in operations had cut these two groups out of the conversation, we would have missed out on valuable insight and run up against enormous resistance to change down the road.

As it was, we had plenty of resistance to get through. These were very big changes. We were asking managers to change the way they thought of the job. Instead of being in control, solving problems, and knowing everything, we wanted them to become mentors, to teach problem solving instead of doing it alone, to make their daily schedules reliable and knowable. And we wanted managers to treat their areas of responsibility as small businesses and to know how much money was going in and out, how resources were being used, and whether their customers were happy. For managers in a not-for-profit hospital, it was a completely different job.

---

8. The A3 is a more detailed version of the plan-do-study-act process defined by W. Edwards Deming. It is the scientific method for problem solving on a single sheet of A3 paper, expanded to include the business context and possible root causes for the problem.

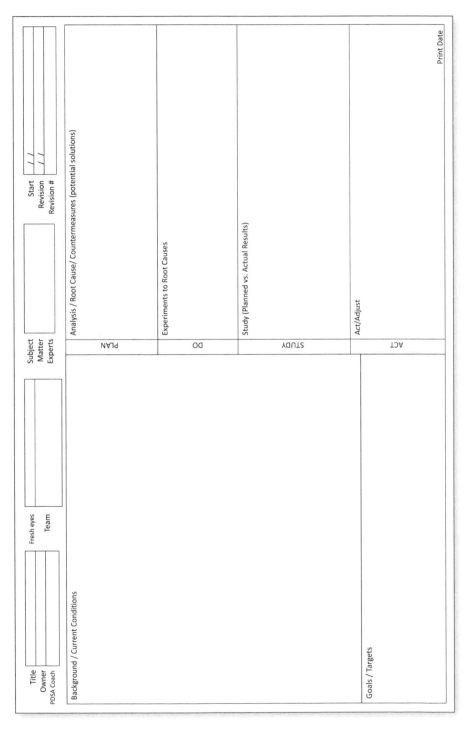

**A3 Template**

We wanted to be careful and deliberate about rolling out these new job descriptions, so we began with a very small alpha group. Really, it was just MaryJeanne Schaffmeyer in obstetrics and Karen Flom in radiation oncology, with their teams acting as our developmental labs. Here is where we tested a two-hour no-meeting zone every morning and began filling in pieces of standard work. A steering committee selected from the August team was observing the experiment on a daily basis, looking at what worked and what did not and rewriting the standard work.

When we felt comfortable with the bones of our new managerial work process, each of us three vice presidents selected two top managers, and then the nine of us went through a 16-week training program that we were also creating along the way. To create our training course, the nine of us separated into what we called writing cells. Each cell was composed of a manager or VP from operations, a lean facilitator, and someone from human resources who together wrote standard work for teaching one of the eight components of what would become our business performance system. When a module was complete, cell members presented their work to one of the developmental labs and got feedback. They reworked and updated the standards and, when the cell members thought the material was about 80% ready, the VP and manager from the developmental lab taught it to the rest of the steering committee to get more feedback. We were still writing and reworking those modules after each of the first two cohorts went through training, each time incorporating feedback to make the courses better. We kept revising and teaching the material to each other until we had trained ourselves to be different leaders.

At the same time, we more clearly defined the A3 as a standardized process to work through problems. Then we hardwired the A3's scientific method into our mentoring and change processes. Meanwhile, human resources was developing a curriculum of core competencies that would be necessary for all ThedaCare leaders, including the ability to develop people, teams, and business acumen, as well as understanding lean tools in management. We committed to incorporating all of HR's thinking on developing leaders as we built the system.

With the time spent in our initial developmental labs, plus training the first alpha group, an entire year flew by. We needed every moment of that, too. Organizations that build upon our work probably will not need to spend an entire week drawing a reverse fishbone or spend months in the laboratory stage trying to define standard work. Re-creating a leadership-management system will not be easy or quick, however. People need time to process big changes, to make mistakes, and to find the right pace.

When the work seems insurmountable, however, think of what you get at the end. At ThedaCare, our leaders do not hide defects or throw problems over the wall hoping someone else with solve them. Managers can talk about the gaps in their unit performance and point out defects as easily as ordering lunch. They can do this because everyone knows that our work consists of closing gaps between our drivers—or goals—and the current-state reality. A favorite saying now is: If you don't have a gap, you don't have a real driver.

We all feel responsible for hitting our targets. But failure to hit the target is not a personal failure. We all know that not meeting the target means rechecking the root cause and finding better countermeasures. Failure belongs to a team or a person, but failure is not a gauge of the worth of a team or a person. It is personal but not judgmental. We have discovered that we can have accountability without blame. For me, this has changed everything.

Next, we will look deeper into the eight interlocking elements of this business performance system, to understand how the system supports the work.

# Chapter 3

# Beginning
## at the Front Line

Before we jump into the components of a business performance system that we *added* to managers' workload, we should note what we subtracted. This is a critical point because, as you read in chapter 2, our managers were stressed to the breaking point. We were talking about adding core competencies and business acumen while many of our managers were struggling with the demands of a continuous improvement organization.

So first, managers needed some immediate relief from the workload. In healthcare, we tend to be addictively additive—we pile on the tasks but are very reluctant to throw anything out. It is like task hoarding. We needed to deselect tasks to make room for new work, but everyone was nervous about this. I was lucky that my boss at the time, Kathryn Correia, who was then president of the hospitals, told me to do what we needed and she would honor our choices. The protected space in which she allowed me and my team to innovate this model was crucial in those early stages.

We also got help from our office of organizational development. Knowing that focusing on the critical few priorities and deselecting extraneous tasks are difficult for any organization, Roger Gerard, our chief learning officer, showed us how to use a series of questions to decide what to deselect. We got together in groups, pulled out our calendars, looked for unnecessary drains on our time, and quickly focused on the sheer number of meetings managers and vice presidents were attending. We asked, "Is this necessary?"

To answer that question, we set a few parameters to judge a meeting's worth. Patient care came first. If the meeting did not involve patient care, it lacked priority. If a meeting's agenda had no stated purpose that related to a manager's sphere of influence, he should do something else instead.

When the other two vice presidents and I were scheduled to be in the same meeting, we got together to decide whether one of us could attend the meeting and share notes with the other two. In studying my own calendar, I had to reassess the content of my work as well as my priorities. In the past, I went to every meeting I was invited to because I thought that was my job. People were showing me respect by inviting me to their meeting, so I should go. Sometimes, that meant I was in a housekeeping meeting for an hour or two while the topic of discussion was the type of product being used to clean the floors. Mere politeness was using up a significant portion of my time. We needed to redefine what it meant to be polite.

In the end, managers and executives all managed to cut down on time spent in meetings by 10%–20% per week. This was a necessary first step, as it turned out, because one of the first things we did in implementing the business performance system was declare that from 8 to 10 a.m. every morning, there would be no scheduled meetings in either of the two major hospitals where we were rolling out the new system.

This no-meeting zone has been key to keeping our business performance system working.

Over the next eight chapters, we will examine each of the elements of our business performance system in detail, since all have been critical in helping us to create a business performance system that is transforming ThedaCare.

Here, I would like to draw a big picture, describing how each element links to the others to create a *system*, not just a pile of discrete tasks. Think of this as the engineering drawings, showing the bare structure of ThedaCare's business performance system and how the elements become interlocking gears.

1.  *Status Reports.* At ThedaCare, we call this a stat sheet meeting, and it is the most transformative element in our system. Short for "status of the business," this conversation, usually between a manager and a supervisor or clinical lead, begins with a series of standardized questions on a single sheet of paper intended to provoke a dialogue about improvement opportunities and roadblocks. This daily, focused discussion about the business, taking place hundreds of times each day with different players all over our hospitals, is the cornerstone of our business performance system. This is about preparedness, about planning our days instead of firefighting our way through them.

2.  *Team Huddle.* Every day, every leader gathers his or her team members into a huddle to widen the conversation about opportunities for improvement, roadblocks, and ongoing projects. This is where we teach and practice standardized problem solving using A3s and the plan-do-study-act cycle and then employ these tools to work through issues and improvements.

3. *Managing to the Established Standard.* This is the discipline of auditing standard work for both clinical and leadership processes in order to keep it from changing or falling to the wayside. By auditing or observing standard work, we also work to spread best practices. It is difficult to maintain any standardized process, clinical or administrative, so auditing must be hardwired into the business performance system and every manager's day. This is where we emphasize that standard work is not a weapon or critique but is the best currently known way to do the work. Standard work is the best practice, and auditing or observing the work is a method for teaching and coaching.

4. *Problem Solving.* We used the A3 or PDSA (plan-do-study-act) as our guide to problem solving with the scientific method. But these tools are as much about mentoring the team on ways to solve problems as they are about finding the best countermeasures for a specific problem.

5. *Transparency.* A visual workplace—where area defects are as visible as team accomplishments—is difficult to establish, but it is the way we keep everyone focused on reality while looking for new opportunity.

6. *Advisory Teams.* For every manager we created a board-of-directors-style team of advisors to help fill in gaps in the manager's areas of expertise and provide fresh perspectives. Advisors might be from finance, human resources, or pharmacy and are responsible for the overall performance of drivers in that area. At ThedaCare, *drivers* refer to the targets or goals on an area's scorecard that lead much of the work of improvement teams. Every unit, clinic, or area has drivers that are tied to the organization's main goals. In general, each advisor on the team "owns" one of the area's drivers and is responsible for understanding problems that affect

performance toward the goal. Advisors may come from inside or outside the manager's area.

7. *Scorecard*. Every manager had a monthly scorecard developed and maintained by the advisory team to help keep track of progress against drivers. The scorecard's vital few metrics help us focus deeply to solve problems and improve performance.

8. *Leadership Standard Work*. This is the most effective weapon available against heroics. When a supervisor, manager, or executive adopts standard work, she promises to be reliable and accountable to her team. Standard work tells the team where a manager will be and when, what questions she will ask and when she will be available to work through issues. According to Toyota, work is standardized when the precise elements of the job are done the same way every time and at a repeatable cycle time. Our stat sheet conversations and huddles are not as precisely timed or repeatable as a mechanized process, so maybe it is more correct to say that our standard work is more like a fixed schedule of activities. We are, however, still evolving, and our goal is a repeatable, reliable system of managing for improvement.

Here is how it all fits together. We use stat sheets to see the business, plan our day, and see the trends developing. We widen the conversation with the team huddle, where we look for trends in performance and use standards to find the gaps between our goals and our performance. This leads directly to problem solving and using the scientific method to close the gaps. Information gathered in huddles and problem solving is then published to the area improvement center—whether that is in an outpatient clinic, an inpatient unit, or a finance office—allowing for transparency so that everyone can monitor progress. The advisory team gathers around the area improvement centers to monitor progress and advise the leader, who monitors the team's performance through the monthly scorecard. Standard work at all levels ensures that everyone stays on track and that we have a measurable norm for leadership performance.

Reduced to seven words, these elements add up to developing people, solving problems, and improving performance.

Now, let's look at the content of the first foundational element: our daily conversations about the business.

# Chapter 4

# Status
## Reports

John was everyone's favorite fixer. A registered nurse with decades of experience, he preferred working nights. John knew every quirk of the units and systems and was always happy to help colleagues in need. Since night shifts are often staffed with newer, less experienced nurses, he was called on often. John[9] was the perfect clinical lead.

At least, he was perfect so long as we were looking for heroes. As ThedaCare hospitals switched our focus to a business performance system that valued standardized processes over heroics, we asked all leaders to focus more on mentoring subordinates to solve their own issues rather than fixing problems for them. And that was what John was doing, he assured his manager. His manager had doubts. John's team was not improving its quality metrics; performance was consistently uneven. Something was wrong.

All leaders in a 24-7 business know the trouble of keeping late-shift personnel aligned with policy. Managers working in administrative

---

9.   As with all first-name-only references, this is a real person whose name I have changed in order to avoid potential embarrassment.

offices tend to work regular business hours and may rarely see the late shift in action for a substantial length of time. Guiding a valued clinical lead toward a different way of leading is difficult to do if guidance is provided only on the rare, rushed occasions when schedules overlap. Luckily, John's manager, Shana Herzfeldt, had a regular in-depth conversation with John hardwired into her standard work.

We call that daily conversation a stat sheet, and it is the foundation of our business performance system. At ThedaCare, a stat sheet, short for "status of the business," refers to both a meeting between a leader and a direct report and the single page of focused questions that guides that 10–20-minute dialogue. Stat sheet questions are intended to help everyone skip past superficial conversations and get to critical information. The stat sheet helps us uncover facts. For Shana Herzfeldt, this daily conversation became her window into the nightly activities of the late shift.

"In this case, we were looking at pneumonia patients that we were tracking to ensure we hit all the quality metrics in the CMS[10] bundle," Shana told me later. "So, every day I was asking John which patients were being tracked. Usually, patients don't need to be tracked for long; we hit all the metrics and they're done. But in this case, he was answering with the same patient room numbers every day."[11]

"So I asked him, 'How are you coaching the nurses on your team on best practices, in order to get the tracking done?' John said he was too busy. I followed up with a few open-ended questions and discovered that he was doing everything—not only his own work but also

---

10. The Centers for Medicare and Medicaid, or CMS, asks hospitals to track certain patients to see that best-practice procedures are carried out. The set of procedures, such as administering aspirin and offering smoking cessation therapy for congestive heart failure patients, is known as a quality bundle.

11. We use room numbers instead of names when discussing patient conditions to comply with HIPPA privacy rules.

correcting problems he saw in his team members' work. It was clear that he thought his work as a clinical lead was to solve the problem rather than coach and mentor his team to solve the problem. When some new fires to fight interrupted his work, the CMS bundle quality measures fell off the list. He was a one-man team."

Lean thinking teaches us that we cannot correct the defects that we cannot see. And it would have taken a very long time to uncover the fact that one very talented, diligent nurse was using heroic measures to cover his entire team on the night shift. We might have eventually noticed that nurses from his team were underprepared for work on other units or on other shifts. But would we have tracked the root cause back to a well-liked clinical lead? The stat sheet helped Shana discover the defect. Then, over the course of a few weeks as she focused her stat sheet questions toward John's mentoring tasks, she helped correct John's course.

"The great thing was that John found his team members really happy to learn the right way to do things. We had mini celebrations when he would report that he coached someone and they were grateful," Shana said. "Now, he's the same well-respected, knowledgeable person that he always was. He just isn't the guy doing everything, and the performance of his team has greatly improved."

The power of the stat sheet lies in the fact that it is a simple, flexible tool to prod two people, usually a manager or supervisor and the clinical lead, into a daily, in-depth conversation about the business in its entirety.[12]

The purpose of the questions and conversation is to help managers understand what is coming at the team today, to see developing trends

---

12. The people involved in a stat sheet meeting can change with the needs of a department and the reality of staffing. ThedaCare managers might meet with a clinical lead or a supervisor or both for a stat sheet, depending on who has time, information, and mentoring needs.

and issues, and to eliminate firefighting in favor of planning ahead. We want to anticipate and react to an emerging problem before it requires emergency response. Knowing that this is the purpose, people understand there is no benefit in glossing over problems. With a business performance system in place, a direct report who answers "fine" or "OK" to stat sheet questions will be counseled on how to spot potential opportunities for improvement.

It is easy to see, then, how the stat sheet is also a teaching tool. By the choice of questions, a leader is constantly showing the subordinate what issues are important. The meeting is a daily opportunity to develop business acumen, while offering the boss an ongoing assessment tool to gauge the team member's critical thinking skills.

Every laboratory, hospital unit, and outpatient clinic has its own questions, but a few things on our stat sheets remain constant. Notice in the example provided below that the first column is divided into six categories. These major categories provide an overview of the business: safety, quality, people (employees), customer service (patients), and cost. The final section, the wrap-up, includes notes on priorities, improvement projects, and causes for celebration.

These categories reflect what everyone needs to understand in order to run their his or her business that day. We need to know that our patients and employees are safe, that we can provide the best possible quality, that we have the right mix of staff on hand, that we can foresee issues that will impact patient satisfaction and well-being, and that we understand what it will cost.

Early in the development of our stat sheet, there was controversy about whether we wanted to talk to our employees about cost. Talking about money is not part of the hospital culture—particularly in a not-for-profit organization. In the end, we decided that we were proud of our

| Unit: Family Birth Center | | | | | | Rev 22 12/22/13 |
|---|---|---|---|---|---|---|
| Daily Measures | M | T | W | T | F | Notes |
| **Safety** | | | | | | M    Huddle Topics |
| What extra safety precautions or staffing measures are in place to keep our staff and patients safe today? | | | | | | |
| Anything happen yesterday that we didn't anticipate? | | | | | | |
| What supply or equipment issues do we have to work through today? | | | | | | |
| **Quality** | | | | | | T    Huddle Topics |
| Immunization Screens Complete _____ Induction Consent _____ Code Cart Sheet _____ | | | | | | |
| What would put us at risk for a patient, family, or provider complaint? | | | | | | |
| K' Board Coaching: What standard work have or will you observe today? | | | | | | |
| What have you learned from your observations of standard work and the coaching that came with it? | | | | | | |
| **People** | | | | | | |
| Tell me about the staffing and experience mix for today and oncoming shifts? What is the plan to support development of today's team? | | | | | | |
| What were the high stress incidents in the last 24 hours? Any staff to debrief with? | | | | | | |
| **Customer Service: Access & Delivery** | | | | | | T    Huddle Topics |
| What is our projected MESH variance and plan? | | | | | | |
| How will you right size your team today either up or down? | | | | | | |
| What is your plan for the next 3 admits? | | | | | | |
| How is TBC capacity and staffing? | | | | | | |
| What will cause barriers to flow today? | | | | | | |
| **Cost** | | | | | | F    Huddle Topics |
| How are assignments affect our productivity target? | | | | | | |
| How will today's work impact our managed expenses? (OT, bonus, extra shifts, TNN, VBACs, sick, lunches, staying past shift end, flexing, RSO, PERIOP, etc) | | | | | | |
| What can be done during downtime today? | | | | | | |
| **Wrap up: Priorities, Improvements & Celebrations** | | | | | | |
| Who has done an extraordinary job recently that we should celebrate? | | | | | | |
| What is your priority today? What is worrying you? | | | | | | |
| How can I help you today? (Share leadership schedule for day) | | | | | | |

**Stat Sheet Family Birth Center Daily**

*For additional stat sheet examples, see appendix figures 3 and 4.*

history of financial stewardship and wanted to spread cost awareness throughout the organization. Since we were working toward developing business acumen in all of our leaders, we would have done them a disservice, I believe, to leave cost out of the equation.

Besides, everyone in healthcare needs to think about cost now. Sweeping changes to healthcare laws mean that most organizations must focus on improving quality and removing costly waste from the system in order to stay afloat. Changing Medicare rules and insurance practices mean that all healthcare providers will need to be business minded now or they may not survive.

This business performance system is not *the* answer to the looming healthcare reimbursement upheavals. It is simply a tool that helps us to see waste and cost for what they are and then cascade that awareness to the front lines. It is a tool to put in place now and use for the long term, but it is not a silver bullet. Healthcare leaders know we will need every tool in the belt to thrive in the changing environment.

Another commonality of all stat sheets at ThedaCare is that all are tied to True North. At ThedaCare, True North refers to the few selected measures that guide our organization strategically. The True North measures are a product of our *hoshin kanri*[13] process, which is where our executive leadership team, in consultation with the board of trustees, agrees on the few critical measures on which to focus our energy. In this way we measure the health of our organization. These measures may change annually or remain constant for years, and they fall into five main categories like navigation points: safety, quality, customer satisfaction, our people, and financial stewardship. Within each of those

---

13. *Hoshin kanri* is a process to help leaders focus their strategy development and deployment. Developed in a few major Japanese companies during the quality movement of the 1950s, hoshin planning is used to select the critical few measures on which to spend an organization's energy.

categories, we have two or three main initiatives on which we focus our improvement activities.

For instance, in 2009 our organization-wide initiatives under the Safety heading were to reduce preventable mortality and medication reconciliation errors. Four years later, following a successful initiative to eliminate medication reconciliation errors, our focus has changed. We still focus on reducing preventable mortality but added a measure to reduce 30-day hospital readmissions.

The shift in focus was visible on our stat sheets. In 2009, managers and vice presidents were typically asking subordinates for any medication reconciliation errors that occurred on the unit the day before and what measures were in place to prevent such errors that day. In 2013, after three years with zero medication reconciliation errors in our hospitals,[14] managers were asking what teams on the unit were doing to identify patients at risk of developing complications and returning to the hospital for the same underlying complaint within 30 days. "Who on your unit is at risk of return?" or "What are you doing today to make sure a patient will not be readmitted within 30 days?" are typical questions.

Notice that these questions are both open-ended and specific because we do not want one-word answers. For instance, in the Manager/Lead Stat Sheet shown on page 35, the first question under the Safety section is not *whether* there are precautions in place to keep patients and staff safe. Surely, there are. Instead, we ask: *Who might get hurt on your unit today? What precautions can we put in place to make sure that does not happen?* Even if the clinical lead scratches her head and says that she cannot

---

14. Medication reconciliation errors, in which patients are incorrectly medicated largely as a result of inaccurate information about what drugs the patient was actually taking, are a major root cause of most patient harm in this country. After ThedaCare redesigned hospital units and work flow, pulling a pharmacist or specially trained pharmacy assistant into all initial patient consultations, we eliminated these errors and, several years later, have maintained a near-zero record.

think of any extra precautions, the question will provoke a conversation about changing needs that might require additional protections.

The final "wrap-up" section is another opportunity for a leader to customize the stat sheet to reflect the unique circumstances of a subordinate and a unit. When a unit has been challenged by more patients than anticipated, for instance, the leader might decide to focus on reasons to celebrate in order to boost morale. If there has been a lot of improvement work in the unit, or new processes need stabilizing, the leader might use all of the "wrap-up" on that topic. Finally, the right-hand column on every stat sheet is where the leader makes notes based on the conversation and identifies which topics, concerns, and improvement ideas will be brought forward to the daily huddle.

To give a sense of our work flow, let me take you through a weekday morning on an inpatient hospital unit. Sometime during the 8–10 a.m. no-meeting zone, the manager will duck into a quiet spot on the unit with the clinical lead. The spot is intentionally public so the rest of the staff and physicians can overhear the conversation; they may even chime in from time to time. Often with a supervisor observing, manager and lead nurse talk through the stat sheet to identify potential issues that might arise on the floor that day. (Managers either have a second meeting with the nursing lead from second shift every day or combine the two meetings into one at shift change.) The manager makes notes and continues through the gemba. The no-meeting zone gives the manager time to check in with his direct reports in order to be prepared for the daily huddle. Once a week or so, the manager will also have a stat sheet conversation with a vice president. All of these conversations may produce new improvement opportunities for discussion within the huddle.

The flexibility of our stat sheets means that we can also use the question-and-answer format to drive improvement. A good example of this began late one night not long ago when I was called at home with an alert that someone had stolen narcotics from an automated drug dispenser[15] in the emergency department. Having taken on the challenge of eliminating incidents of missing drugs from our hospitals, I had asked that security notify me immediately whenever drugs disappeared—no matter the hour. By the time I got to Appleton Medical Center in the morning, I had a plan to investigate using stat sheets.

First, I pulled together a huddle of the three vice presidents who report to me and briefed them on the incident. One troubling issue, besides the missing narcotic, was that we could only narrow down the suspect list as far as three people. We did not know for sure who took the drugs. So we went to gemba together to look at an automated drug dispenser and ask a few questions. Then I asked my team of VPs to put new questions about use of drug-dispensing machines on all of their stat sheets and ask their managers to do the same. We wanted managers to ask their direct reports for a description of the standard work surrounding use of the drug dispensers.

Within a week, we compiled the intelligence and had a clear view of the wide variances in standard work around getting narcotics. Every unit pulled drugs and wasted[16] drugs in a different fashion. One floor of the hospital might require two separate security log-ins to get narcotics dispensed, while another might need one.

Following a report of findings, my team pulled together an ad hoc team from multiple hospital units in order to write one standard for all drug dispensers and spread it throughout the hospitals. With the

---

15. There are many brands of automated drug-dispensing machines available and in use in hospitals, but all operate on the same premise of securing drugs until they are dispensed and then recording information about what was dispensed when and to whom.

16. The term "wasted" is used for all drug disposals, whether because of expiration or overage. Overage is common. Every time a specific amount of drug is dispensed, whether in liquid or pill form, that which is not used is reconciled against how much was used, and any leftovers are disposed of or wasted.

new standard work, everyone knew that we would be able to quickly pinpoint exactly which employee had pulled which drugs for what purpose. In the six months following that incident, we had no more reported incidents of missing narcotics from the dispensers.[17]

Our simple stat sheet can also be a great leadership shortcut, as former manager Michael Radtke told me. Mike is one of those really likeable, talented caregivers that seemed a natural leader from the beginning. So, he did not need management training, right? Somehow, in spite of our training neglect, Mike kept rising through the ranks, moving around fairly often while still being unsure of his real leadership skills.

After managing a few departments, Mike did a three-year rotation through the ThedaCare Improvement System office. He worked as a facilitator there and was one of many who helped develop our business performance system. He knew about standard work for managers, stat sheets, and huddles. Still, when he finished his lean facilitator rotation and was named interim manager of a hospital inpatient unit, he was nervous.

We all know that feeling. On your first day leading a new area, people tend to stare at you like you are the new kid in the third grade of a small school—only now you are the boss. There is nothing worse than being in charge and feeling like an extra, not-very-useful limb.

What Mike discovered that day was that he had secret weapons: his predecessor's stat sheet and knowledge of standard work. He was in the office at 6:30 a.m., and by the time he hit gemba at 7 a.m., he was ready.

"It was such a relief to be on the unit my very first day and know exactly what I was doing," Mike said. "I wasn't just walking around saying, 'How are you doing?' or waiting until the end of the month to

---

17. A complete A3 detailing our experiments in reducing drug diversions is available in the appendix, figure 9.

find out how we were doing. I knew what questions to ask and what was important on this unit. I was there, fully integrated, from day one."

Mike is now director of diagnostic imaging for the system,[18] which puts him between managers and vice presidents in the hierarchy, and he is still finding the value—and the struggle—in the discipline of standard work for leaders. Not long ago he was telling me that he had been through a very busy stretch and dropped his stat sheet conversations with his managers for a while. The managers who report to him would probably appreciate the break, he thought. Not exactly.

"We were in a meeting and a manager told me, point blank, if I stopped asking her those questions, she was going to stop asking questions of her team. She needed me to keep her on track," Mike said. "It made me see this system as a whole tiered structure of accountability. It's easy to lose sight of the importance of that shared accountability. If our standard work was not linked together the way it is, I could have really dropped the ball."

So, stat sheets are a leader's shortcut. They offer structure to our morning rounds. They are a format for organizing improvement work. They are also a teaching tool and an ongoing performance assessment device. They are a daily conversation between two people focused on the business at hand, multiplied throughout the organization. The stat sheet is a profoundly simple and powerful tool. On its own, however, the impact of the stat sheet would be limited. What we need is to involve a larger team to solve larger problems. So, on to the huddle.

---

18. Since Mike is a director for the entire ThedaCare system, he does not appear on the organizational chart for the hospitals. His position, however, is commensurate to a VP.

# Chapter 5

# The Huddle

Jennifer Fredriksen's team was pretty quiet for the first couple of months. Every morning just after 9 a.m. in the spring of 2010, the early days of our business performance system, they would gather around a huddle board parked in a discreet hallway in Theda Clark Medical Center's Family Birth Center. Jen would talk through improvement ideas and discuss barriers they might face that day. The team seemed interested enough; they just did not speak up much. In addition to the five or six nurses, there were usually a couple of educators[19] present, and sometimes someone from staffing or housekeeping joined the huddle, depending on who Jen thought would add value to the discussion. I would often join them, too, in my role as vice president.

Maybe the presence of outsiders kept the unit nurses reticent, Jen thought. She worried about the quiet but kept plugging away at those 15-minute huddles—showing new metrics, updating improvement projects, talking about how the projects were tied to drivers (targets for

---

19. Like most large health systems, ThedaCare has an education department to keep personnel up-to-date on the latest technology and best practices. Educators who work in that department are most often nurses who discovered a talent for teaching.

improvement) and our True North, and prioritizing new improvement ideas with her team. Jen was not sure how much of this business talk her team was taking in but decided she would trust the process.

One day about six months after the daily huddles began, they were talking about their quality driver and a new experiment to improve performance. The driver was surgical site infections. Their goal, of course, was to eliminate them. And after a year of observing dozens of Cesarean sections; tracking results; and experimenting with possible causes such as equipment, materials used, and changing surgical prep work, the team was steadily pushing the trend line down.

"We've had a suggestion from [one of our physicians] to experiment now with a new surgical drape," Jen told the group that morning. "The idea is that this different drape may further reduce risk of infection. What does everyone think about that?"

There were a couple of comments about the drapes, how they worked, and why they might be better. While the team was talking about how the drapes might reduce risk of infection, a staff nurse standing a little back from the others raised a tentative hand and said, "Are these more expensive than the ones we currently use?"

It was a simple question, but those words sent a little thrill through Jen and me; it was the sign of growing business acumen in the nursing staff. And it seemed to be unforced, a natural outgrowth of these daily discussions.

Jen answered that the new drapes were nearly identical in price and then later told me that she had been thinking about her own days on the floor as a nurse. In those days, they all attended bimonthly staff meetings, and during one brief section, someone would get up and scribble hospital financials on a flip chart. That was it.

"Cost was never part of my thinking back then," Jen said. "I wanted whatever would make things easier for me and better for my patient. Finances were never connected to the day-to-day work."

Frontline nurses making that connection between daily decisions and system costs are just one reason that the huddle started as an experiment but became an integral part of our business performance system. We find more reasons to like the huddle every day. This in-depth, stand-up, daily group discussion has become a source of peer-to-peer training, knowledge sharing, team building, and continuous improvement—all with a time commitment of 15–20 minutes per day. Many groups keep a clock on the huddle board to keep everyone aware of the standing commitment to brevity.

Before we go into depth on the structure and appearance of a good huddle, let me describe the advantages of maintaining the structure and schedule discipline of these daily meetings. I could easily reel off a dozen benefits, but my top three are engagement, team problem solving, and communication.

By "engagement" I am referring not just to employees feeling involved, but also to peer-to-peer interactions that lead naturally to skill and leadership development. Let me illustrate. One day I was in a huddle in an oncology unit and a nurse asked to talk about a syringe that was frequently used on the unit. It was a bad product, the nurse said; we really should stock something else. In the old days, this is exactly the kind of complaint that would have been thrown at the manager to handle. The manager would have been expected to investigate, experiment, and introduce a new product—if he or she had the time. But this time, another nurse in the huddle asked why the first nurse did not like the syringe. A third nurse talked about the different syringes they had tried in the past for that application and the problems they encountered. A fourth nurse suggested a slightly different approach to try when using the syringe, and the group—including the first nurse—agreed to try this approach as an experiment. Even though other nurses had not experienced the same trouble, all agreed it was an experiment that might help everyone.

This kind of team problem solving is an unheard-of luxury in most hospitals, where running from one emergency to the next—many of our own making—is the norm and problems are "solved" by one hero on the fly. But we have discovered that when teams of people with diverse skills gather to consider a problem, we can see the issue from many vantage points and have the opportunity to truly address the root cause and anticipate the ramifications of our actions.

For instance, when one surgical unit realized that team members were always hunting for surgical gloves inside the O.R., the team agreed on the need for standardized glove placement in every O.R. In the huddle, they had enough points of view to quickly identify the one centrally located pole in their identical operating rooms that was the best place to mount the glove boxes. Of course, they ran an experiment first before putting the standard in place, but their confidence in the solution was the result of being able to examine the issue from many angles at once.

Finally, team communication is a huge benefit of these daily huddles. Here, administrative assistants are given equal voice with registered nurses, senior executives, and physicians as they work together to identify problems and find countermeasures. In every huddle, we also look for opportunities to celebrate—not just improvements but also new babies, graduations, and life goals. Every huddle underscores the fact that we are teams, trusting one another and dependent on each other to save lives and restore health to our patients.

Yes, it requires commitment and discipline to get these benefits, but the huddle can offer enormous time savings, too. Just consider what the

huddle does for our hospitalist group. This is a group of 15 physicians—
the doctors in charge of general inpatient medical care in our units—and
six advanced practitioners such as physician assistants and nurse practitioners. Because of the providers' schedules, they huddle once a week
instead of every day, and those weekly huddles take 20–40 minutes.
Hospitalists have regular meetings for clinical issues as well; the huddles
are reserved for trouble-shooting processes and system improvements.

"One place I really see a difference now is in the email chains. They
used to be massive and time-consuming," Jill Menzel, manager of the
hospitalist program and co-leader of the hospitalists' huddle, told me.
"Before, you might have one physician with a problem, and she might
email everybody in the group about it. Then someone would reply to
everyone, and soon you had this massive email chain where voices were
getting lost and the problem was never fully examined."

Now, if a physician has a problem because, for instance, a clinical team
is not ready to do the patient rounds when he arrives on the floor,
he can bring the issue to the huddle. There, we can find out if other
doctors have the same complaint, whether the solution needs to be system-wide or unit-specific, and how we might alter or create standard
work to address the problem.

In years past, a manager such as Jill might have been compelled to fix
a problem raised by Provider A only to find that his solution created a
problem for Provider B's work flow. Trying to juggle the needs of 21
providers spread over two hospitals and several inpatient units meant
a manager could veer around wildly for days trying to solve a simple
problem while the email chains exploded. Pulling everyone together
once a week to solve problems together has dramatically changed that
dynamic and saved everyone a lot of time.

Another advantage I see in our stand-up huddles is that individuals regularly volunteer to take responsibility for tackling a problem and then commit to a time line for finishing the project or reporting back to the group about roadblocks. The social pressure of making that promise to your colleagues is very strong. As a result, tasks and projects are completed with greater frequency, and trust builds within the group.

"We make priorities as a team, talk out the problems, and find answers. We are not going down a rabbit hole because someone has the loudest voice," Jill says.

A well-run huddle can appear casual, even loose. It is anything but. Experience has taught us that a huddle is most effective when it is standardized, follows a precise and well-known formula, and is organized around improvement projects—updates, new ideas, and talking through problems with the benefit of many different points of view and types of experience.

In ThedaCare hospitals, we firmly believe in standardization. All of our huddle boards look alike so that anyone—team member, hospital management, even casual observer—can see at a glance how the team is performing. We try to adhere to the five-five rule: anyone should be able to get a complete picture of the area's progress in five seconds by looking at the board from five feet away.

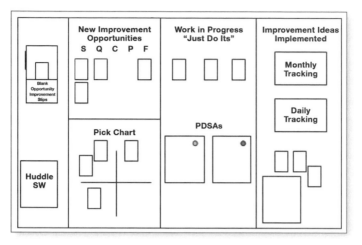

**Huddle Board**

*For a detailed view of our standard work to create a huddle board, see appendix figure 5.*

Posted on every board is the standard work for a huddle—the huddle's agenda—so that everyone knows what to expect and anyone could run the huddle at a moment's notice. The huddle agenda is always the same, but that does not mean that every item gets equal weight every day. The leader begins with a review of all improvement work in progress. This might be a quick look at fast-action fixes (we call them *just do its*) or a more in-depth look at a complicated PDSA or A3 that has hit a snag.[20] All A3s on the board are labeled with either a green dot, meaning work is progressing smoothly, or a red dot, meaning that we have hit a snag that needs untangling. Completed projects are moved to the appropriate area of the board.

Next, the team reviews any new improvement opportunities and prioritizes those new projects using a PICK chart. (See appendix figure 6

---

20. PDSA, or plan, do, study, act, is the format that ThedaCare hospitals use for an A3 improvement project. The terms are sometimes used interchangeably, and, in the generic, both simply mean "improvement project," but PDSA is the process we use to work through experiments. More about that in chapter 7.

for a PICK chart, followed by an example of a New Improvement Opportunity form, figure 7.) Sometimes called a decision matrix or impact analysis chart, the PICK initials stand for the four quadrants that help categorize projects by difficulty and impact.

> Possible: low impact, low difficulty

> Implement now: high impact, low difficulty

> Challenge: high impact, more difficult

> Kibosh: low impact, high difficulty

We are careful to talk through any improvement suggestion that lands in Kibosh, of course, as we do not want to discourage people from offering ideas. Also, we do not leave New Improvement Opportunity slips in the Kibosh quadrant. Instead, the manager has a separate conversation with the person who proposed the project to more fully discuss and evaluate the idea. This is a teaching opportunity; we never want to embarrass anyone.

Then, the huddle leader briefly reviews the *area improvement center*. This is the board that shows each of the drivers, or major improvement targets, for the area and up-to-date metrics showing progress of the projects toward the goal.

The final agenda item is always the celebration, for improvements realized or personal milestones achieved by team members and their families.

The daily huddle is attended by the area manager and whoever is available on the unit or the clinic, plus any outsiders who may have input, such as housekeepers, finance experts, educators, or clinicians in the upstream or downstream flow of patients. Rarely, we have noticed a unit staff member ducking huddles and have a private word with that person to request that they add their voice to the team. Most of the time, people are happy to attend because they know that huddles directly affect the content of their work.

If the unit manager is not available to run the huddle, she makes sure that one of her supervisors is prepared to run the daily meeting. In mature areas where the business performance system has been in place for a while and running smoothly, any willing staff person is able to pick up the standard work and run a huddle.

Quite often, a vice president, the COO, or I drop by to observe a huddle in progress. The vice presidents and I decide on Monday morning which huddles we will attend that week, based on areas of emerging need. Or, in the absence of pressing need, we let a scheduled rotation be our guide.

The huddle board is also standardized and made up of six major areas. An illustration is shown in the appendix, figure 5.

1.  *Forms.* This lane has two pockets: one for blank New Improvement Opportunity forms and one for the huddle standard work.

2.  *New Improvement Opportunities.* This lane has a parking lot for New Improvement Opportunity forms, organized by category—safety, quality, customer loyalty, people, and financial stewardship—and the PICK Chart to help us prioritize new opportunities.

3.  *Work in Progress.* This lane includes the quick projects and the more in-depth A3 or PDSA projects.

4.  *Improvement Ideas Implemented.* This is where all finished projects land, giving the team a constant visual reminder of their accomplishments. A manager or supervisor also reviews

the New Improvement Opportunity slips parked here every month to ensure sustainment.

5. *Area Improvement Center.* This is often a separate board. At the top is a single sheet showing ThedaCare's True North and then five or more columns for the important charts and collected data related to the area's drivers. If a unit driver is to eliminate surgical site infections, for instance, this lane will contain a PDSA and the charts that track progress toward the goal such as historical data, daily tracking, and Pareto[21] charts that show what defects are being measured and the frequency of occurrence. We try to configure charts so that positive trends are shown by upward sweeps to the right of the graph so it is easy to see whether the reported metrics are up-to-date.

6. *Celebrations.* This is where we include everything we can celebrate, including accomplishments toward a goal, positive comments from patients or providers, defect removal, waste reduction, and personal achievements.

The huddle board is a constant, public reminder of our commitment to the business performance system. That means the information should be fresh and well organized and show how the team is working together to address issues in the unit or clinic.

As our teams become more sophisticated in the use of lean tools such as PDSAs, our huddle agendas will change. I look forward to the day when our people yearn to move into more depth. Instead of chasing defects, we should be able to use our huddles to think about improving standards. Maybe we can start thinking creatively about controlling glucose levels, for instance, or new ways to educate patients about

---

21. A Pareto chart is most often a vertical bar graph in which instances of defects or actions are plotted in decreasing order of frequency from left to right. It is used to help teams quickly see what problem or action happens most often.

avoiding infections. When that happens, when we are ready for the huddles of tomorrow, you can be sure we will write new standard work first and hew to a standardized format.

We will do this because we have learned that without standards, we are all at risk of drift—of undermining the interconnected work of the business performance system through a failure to follow our process every time. This is hard work, but following our standard method and spreading best practices are absolutely necessary. And that brings us to our next element of the business performance system: managing to the established standard.

# Chapter 6

# Managing
## to the Standard

Every lean organization knows this: standardizing a process is the critical first step toward improving it. Without standardization, there can be no improvement. As W. Edwards Deming pointed out, only a consistent, standard process permits us to see inherent errors. In hospitals, we see the power of this idea all the time. Think about a series of people arriving in the emergency room with chest pains. If we treat each one differently—with EKGs and other diagnostic tests given randomly each time—it is nearly impossible to pinpoint why some patients wait an hour for life-saving treatments while others are treated in 20 minutes. Without consistency, every error—every time a patient is harmed by waiting too long for treatment or getting the wrong medicine—seems unique, and we respond with a new workaround or quick fix, further obscuring the true nature of the problem.

We know this, too: writing standard work is a lot easier than getting people to consistently follow it. Standards can be as slippery as loose mercury once humans are involved. People like to change things up; we like to personalize our work, to stamp it with our unique insights into the process. Sometimes, we are just too busy to look up the standard. As a result, from the moment it is written, standard work is under constant threat of a sideways drift.

Organization-wide discipline is required to keep everyone following the major steps in a standardized sequence, and to have those standards rewritten by teams when improvements or corrections are needed. It is up to leaders to help their teams follow and improve the standard work through observation and auditing people as they work through standard processes. But auditing standard work is a task that always seems so much less important than, well, anything else. This is why we have hardwired this duty into our leadership standard work and the business performance system.

Every day, leaders throughout our hospitals drop in on huddles and stat sheet meetings to observe work and to mentor direct reports on maintaining the standard work of the business performance system. We also maintain a steady cadence of observing clinical work to ensure best practices are in place. We have found that observing both types of processes, management and clinical, is imperative. We call this managing to the standard. It is written into every leader's standard work and we have found that it has been effective in ways we never expected.

Consider one example from the emergency department at Appleton Medical Center from the early days of the business performance system. COO MaryJeanne Schaffmeyer was a vice president of hospital operations at the time and mentoring the excellent manager of that department, Peggy Bree. MaryJeanne would drop by the E.D. at least once a week to look at the huddle boards and often found Peggy's name on nearly every improvement item and to-do list. Instead of teaching and mentoring, Peggy was trying to fix what came up. It is a common problem. MaryJeanne counseled Peggy on encouraging other people to take the lead and to teach instead of do.

One day, MaryJeanne was observing the E.D. huddle when a fairly complicated issue was put forward for improvement. From the time a patient in an emergency department is determined to require admission to the hospital until that patient arrives to a bed on an inpatient unit—we can call this "time to bed"—is an important measure. Delays in this handoff can create jams in the E.D., lead to a lag in care being administered, and decrease patient satisfaction. Nobody wants drugs or procedures delayed at this important juncture, yet this time-to-bed measure is a vexing problem in many hospitals.

Peggy, having been coached about getting other people to take the lead, gamely asked the huddle whether anyone would like to lead a team investigation of this critical handoff and then write the standard work for a better process. The hand that shot up belonged to a young administrative assistant.

"I'll do it," she said. "I want to."

Peggy paused. For all her enthusiasm, the assistant would be at a disadvantage, Peggy thought. She was a firecracker but did not have the same education level as the others; she might be perceived as lacking necessary status. How could she lead a full kaizen team project like this, which required coordination across hospital units? Peggy would need to delegate her authority and offer plenty of coaching; she was not at all sure this young woman could lead a team. On the other hand, Peggy's boss was standing there watching her. And Peggy was supposed to be encouraging others to lead.

"Tell me why you want to take on this project," Peggy said with a smile.

"Well, I know the admission process and I am the one who is sitting behind the front desk, watching people waiting for their beds in the units," the young woman, whom we will call Julie, said. "I'd like to help."

Julie had a good point. So, Peggy became the project sponsor, and the young administrative assistant was named team leader. We backfilled Julie's position behind the front desk to allow her to devote time to learning new skills. Peggy helped her think about putting together a cross-functional kaizen team and then keeping everyone on track to find the best way to standardize and improve the process. Julie assembled her team, learned new tools such as gap analysis and how to run time studies, and coordinated with at least two other hospital units. When her team was finished, they had created a process that had every patient going from emergency room to a bed in a unit in 20 minutes or less. Her team had written the standard work and taught the process to others.

At a subsequent huddle, Peggy asked who might be willing to observe the new time-to-bed standard work to gather performance data. Guess whose hand shot up? It was not just Julie's. Half a dozen people volunteered. Julie had so impressed her colleagues with her enthusiasm for the project that there was now real interest in observing this rather mundane yet critical process.

"In lean work, improvement is the exciting thing. We all know that. Making it stick is harder," MaryJeanne says now. "This project—with Peggy reaching out for new leaders and an assistant's enthusiasm spreading like that—showed us that if you build a team that is invested in the standard, they will make it stick because they have been directly involved in creating it."

The time-to-bed project took place in early 2011. Since then, the process has been revisited a number of times, improved, and the standard work rewritten. That is the nature of improvement. And at every iteration, the new standard work needed to be repeatedly observed, and people needed to be coached on creating and maintaining the standard. It sounds a bit dull, but MaryJeanne and leaders like her know that sticking to this method of process improvement creates enormous opportunities for the organization.

"There is nothing dynamic about coaching standard work unless you're coaching in such a way that it develops people," MaryJeanne says. "We use standard work observations to help people build technical and leadership skills and also to help them understand the value of standards. They must want to make standardization work."

We know we need standard work in order to avoid the chaos of many people performing the same process in many different ways, which creates variation and the need for workarounds. We need to be able to pick up the tool we need, when we need it. We need to trust that everyone has the same idea of how a task gets done.

We also know that people can react negatively to the idea of standard work. The terms "cookbook medicine" and "robot" may get tossed around when we tell people we want everyone to do a task or procedure in the same way. Introduce the idea that we intend to determine and, when appropriate, the amount of time a step should take and the language can get a lot worse. So the first thing we need to do is identify what work should be standardized—which task sequences should be decided by a team and then be considered unchangeable except by team decision—and what work is best left to individual decision without need for team agreement.

One side of the answer is simple: we must standardize any process that we want to improve. Processes that are good candidates for standardization tend to be multistep administrative or clinical procedures. What we do not standardize tends to be either simpler or more complex. We do not tell people how to pick up a pen, for instance, and we cannot standardize the way a trauma surgeon works on an unconscious patient who is barely clinging to life. In fact, many common surgeries such as mastectomies or cardiac bypasses cannot be standardized across our hospitals because surgeons have learned vastly different techniques for the same procedures during postgraduate training. We can standardize the processes and equipment around a procedure for knee replacements, for instance, but we cannot—and should not—dictate the precise angle of the surgeon's knife. Nor should standards be followed slavishly in the face of unusual circumstances.

ThedaCare's CEO Dean Gruner tackled this issue in his monthly letter to employees when he wrote in 2013 that standard work does not replace critical thinking. Blindly following standard work in the face of the variations that are inevitable in patient care is just as potentially harmful as having no standards at all. He wrote:

> Mindfulness implies that we are anticipating what might go wrong and are taking action to lower that risk. The standard might be followed, but what if the patient has other conditions that should be considered? . . . Yes we should create standard work, reduce unnecessary variation and work to improve the standard work after it is created. But don't be a robot! Use your powers of observation and critical thinking to sense when problems are occurring and need action.

Autonomy versus standardization is no simple issue, and it can be used as cover for people who simply do not like change. Clinicians who want to avoid standardization can decide that deviation from the standard is warranted 85% of the time. Those who see the value of lean thinking may see exceptions to the standard just 15% of the time. We will be having arguments about this for some time into the future, but I contend that they are arguments worth having. As we prove that standardized processes—such as the ones that eliminated medication reconciliation errors in our inpatient units—are better for hospitals and patients alike, we will move more physicians into the "believer" column.

Processes that can be standardized are agreed upon by improvement teams. A team writes the standard onto work sheets and then trains unit or clinic staff on performing to the standard. While staff is being trained, standard work sheets describing the proper methods for performing the work are usually displayed in a common area. When staff members display competence, the work sheets are usually taken down and a copy of the standard work is stored on a computer drive that all can access. Staff members new to the unit are trained in all written standards by the supervisor or clinical leads. In a few instances, standard work is printed, laminated, and posted for long periods. This is impractical in most instances because of the sheer volume of work sheets, but there have been exceptions for critical processes in high-volume areas. And then there is another step to making standard work stick.

Once we have identified what needs to be standardized, with processes written and people trained, we are ready to put the standard work on an observation calendar board, the *kamishibai*. Translated from the Japanese as "paper theater," kamishibai is a picture board that was used by itinerant storytellers in Japan who adopted the method of illustrating stories for an audience from the practice of twelfth-century Buddhist monks. Think of the old felt boards used by elementary school teachers and you have the picture. In a lean organization, kamishibai boards are visual cues and controls for performing audits of standard work.

A kamishibai tells the stories of how tasks should be accomplished and tells when those tasks will be observed. At ThedaCare, the board consists very simply of a large calendar; a pouch to hold written standard work, usually in a binder; and a pouch for cards with the names of standardized processes to be observed. In our hospitals, about 80% of the cards are for clinical standard work, also called best practices, and 20%

show a management process, such as teaching a lean tool or mentoring someone in problem-solving techniques.

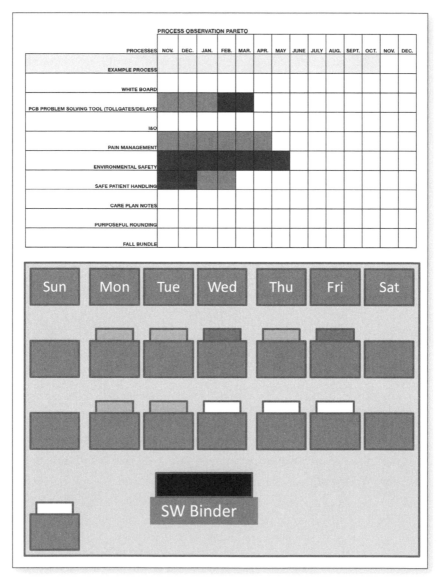

**Kamishibai Board / Process Observation Standard Work**

*Our standard work for creating a Kamishibai board is in the appendix, figure 8.*

The calendar has small pockets for every day of the week, and the manager of that unit or clinic, who also owns the kamishibai, loads those pockets with cards for processes to be observed. If a procedure is complicated and lengthy, the day's slot might have only one card describing that sequence of standard work. More than one card in a slot usually means the procedures can be done in a short time, such as drawing blood or wrapping a new baby in a blanket. Clinical standard work is rooted in Milliman Guidelines, which are evidence-based best practices for a range of medical conditions and chronic illnesses, adopted widely throughout the United States.

Peer-to-peer observation within the work team is the ideal method for this task, especially in a mature lean hospital. But we find that being watched and feeling judged by one's peers can be emotionally fraught. In healthcare, clinicians are accustomed to being watched while they work since doctors and nurses are frequently observed for competency in their early years on the job. However, they expect that observation to be conducted by a more senior person in their specialization. It is difficult for people to accept coaching from team members who might be at the same or a somewhat lower professional level. So, at this point, managers do the majority of standard work auditing, and it is a task on every manager's daily standard work. Supervisors and vice presidents fill in where they can or where their expertise is needed.[22]

The manager/observer begins by selecting a card from the day's pocket, observes the clinical or leadership procedure, and affixes a green dot to the card if it was performed as written in the standard work. A red dot means a step was skipped or incorrectly done. Red dots are a sign that people are drifting away from standard work, and we place the dots in such a way that we know what step was observed as incorrect or skipped. Both red and green dots end up on Pareto charts that are reviewed at

---

22. As of this writing, kamishibai boards do not include observations of physicians' work.

monthly leadership meetings for discussion of potential countermeasures, whether that means retraining on the standard work or improving it.

Can an organization keep standard work and clinical best practices from drifting without the discipline of a kamishibai board and frequent audits? Maybe, but our history suggests that it is unlikely. Before the business performance system brought us kamishibai boards, we did what most hospitals do: we informed clinicians of currently known best practices and changes in the Milliman Guidelines. Sometimes we got an educator out on the floor to demonstrate procedures and then moved on to the next case. Leaders were too often surprised, six months later, to find that variation was more standard than adherence to the best practice.

"Kamishibai radically changed the leader's role," says Jill Case-Wirth, our chief nursing officer and a healthcare leader for 26 of her 30 years in nursing. "Once our clinicians knew leaders weren't playing whack-a-mole on people for not following standard work—once they knew that we were learning to see, too—observations became the basis for a conversation rather than a confrontation.

"Over my career, we have made an awful lot of changes to procedures, but very few became standard clinical practices," Jill says. "This is the first time that I'm confident that critical changes we need to make are actually sticking and not just drifting away."

During those conversations on the floor, when leaders saw that standard work was not being followed, we were looking for the root cause of drift. If the nurses were consistently skipping step six in the baby-wrapping standard work, for instance, and neglecting to tuck in the baby's feet, the leader was not just slapping a red dot on the card and walking away.

"We make sure we talk with the clinician while observing," MaryJeanne Schaffmeyer says. "We might say, 'I really like the way you snuggled the baby and smiled at her. I'm just wondering why you didn't do step six and tuck in her feet. Was it hard to do within the available time? Or did it feel wrong? Why?"

This conversation was not just one-on-one between observer and observed. The kamishibai board with its Pareto chart also meant that the area vice president or COO could walk by and tell at a glance whether babies' feet were being left unwrapped and ask why. We have found that leaders at every level have unique insights to offer in the arena of standard work, once they can see the issues.

Observing work and talking about where we fail to follow standards should not feel like judgment and confrontation as long as everyone recognizes that a certain amount of drift from standard work and best practices is as natural as a change in the weather. This is why we go to the trouble to audit or observe, because we want to be aware of any changes and to take quick action for the benefit of patients and providers alike. It is up to an organization's top leadership to deliver this message, in person and frequently.

I have made it a habit to check a number of kamishibai boards with my team on a regular basis. And each time we look at a board or pull cards and observe the work, we try to repeat the message that standard work is critically important. When frontline caregivers are not following standards, we need to know why for the sake of our patients.

Being there and delivering that message is a task that executives cannot delegate. We know that we need to model the behaviors we want to see and that every interaction on the floor is a teaching opportunity. This is the glue that holds our system together. We develop the standard, teach the standard, and then manage to the standard.

Once we had standards locked in place at ThedaCare, we could move on to improving the system with problem solving via the scientific method. We will see how in the next chapter.

# Chapter 7

# Problem
## Solving

Mike Vela never could look away, not knowing what he knew. Hired by ThedaCare as the medication safety officer in 2008, it was his job to know the rules for handling and disposing all drugs, whether toxic or benign. He saw violations everywhere.

He knew that, according to the 1970 Federal Resource Conservation and Recovery Act, the popular blood-thinning drug Coumadin could be thrown away only into a black bucket and that once the drug accumulated past a certain weight or a certain date, it had to be picked up by a specialty company that would burn it twice—once for the drug, once for the ashes. It was not just the drug; anything that touched the drug, such as the little cups used to carry pills to the patient, was supposed to be burned twice, too. Most everyone knew that Coumadin required special handling, but those little paper cups could easily escape notice. There were also heavy metals such as selenium that hospitals had to dispose of properly, which can be a daunting task when you know that selenium is, for instance, common in dandruff shampoo and that anything left over in a bottle needed special handling.

Mike was the roving expert, calling out violations in the units, helping the pharmacy change the way it compounded certain elements, teaching people to double glove when necessary. He knew he was responsible for keeping people safe, but sometimes, he confided to me later, he felt like a disruptive force, the guy who might interrupt important improvement work to cite an obscure regulation.

Then Mike was tapped to fill in as interim pharmacy manager, and first thing, we asked him to attend business performance system training. For 16 weeks, he studied problem solving, data collection, stat sheets, and mentoring—the whole system. He and his classmates identified problems, but nobody was allowed to take independent action. They were supposed to mentor others instead. Mike thought he might twitch right out of his skin.

"I realized that I was a firefighter. I had the answer for everything. I knew every regulation and who wrote it," Mike told me. "But going through the management training, that's when I saw the value of finding the big picture instead of fighting every fire."

And then in his first six months as interim pharmacy manager, there was a severe drug shortage after a manufacturer announced it would stop producing 84 elements used in compounding drugs. Mike jumped in as though he had never gone through business performance training, working 12-hour days to ensure medications were available and leaving his team behind. In the face of an emergency, he went right back to firefighting. Some reflexes are really hard to change.

Later that winter, another shortage hit the hospitals, and a fellow manager took Mike aside and asked, "Are you going to be that guy again—the guy who comes in at 6 a.m., stays until 7 p.m., and does everything himself? Or, are you going to set up a process?"

That rocked Mike back on his heels. He knew, intellectually, that leading his team to create standard work to deal with drug shortages as they came up was the right thing to do. It was just so hard not to leap in with all the answers. This time, though, he assembled the team and followed his leadership standard work to help the team create its standard work for these inevitable emergencies. The team identified the critical questions to ask as they worked through an A3 in order to find the best countermeasures for drug shortages. They created standardized action plans, and Mike was willing to admit that he thought it went OK.

The test came the following autumn, and Mike will never forget it. He was in the backyard playing with his kids in the late afternoon when he got a telephone call from a quality manager. Had Mike been following news about the outbreak of fungal meningitis cases? News had just broken that contaminated epidural steroid injections had been traced back to the New England Compounding Center in Framingham, Massachusetts, the manager said. Did ThedaCare hospitals get any drugs from there?

Mike's heart leapt into his throat. "I called my team immediately and found them already in the process of working through the standard steps we had written for this kind of situation. I guess I sounded pretty alarmed because Wendy said, 'Don't worry, Mike; we got this.' This was an emergency, and they were calmly, methodically working through the A3 and standard work that we wrote," Mike said.

This is a perfect illustration of two principles about problem solving being true at once: using the scientific method to problem solve is about confronting and addressing safety and quality issues and it is equally about developing people. Both attacking problems and developing people are the equal end goals of this process.

Before we get into the use of problem solving to develop people, however, we should address the actual A3 problem-solving process. In the lean world, I have noticed people sometimes become stuck on the labels for methods used to work through problems. I like to tell people that whether you call it A3, PDSA, or PDCA (plan, do, *check*, act), what matters is that it is rooted in the scientific method and that people understand and reflexively use the chosen method.

At ThedaCare, we refer to problem solving as PDSA—the continuing cycle of plan, do, study, act—and we want everyone to instinctively use it when thinking about problems, opportunities, or new initiatives. But that is just one piece of the puzzle. PDSA is the way we think about addressing problems or opportunities, and then we use A3 as the context. An A3-sized sheet of paper is an artifact of the team's problem solving—where ideas and actions are written—but the A3 also spurs us to provide greater depth and detail.

Using the A3, teams are guided to grasp the whole situation, including background and current conditions, and then boil the problem or opportunity down into a single well-defined statement. (The caution here is that a solution should not be part of the problem statement.) Here is an example of a real problem statement from an obstetrics A3 regarding problems in getting a fairly common postpartum drug to women in need:

> Currently on the units (of both hospitals), the Rhogam administration and documentation process requires nurses to leave the floor for 12 min. walking 1/4 mile to be able to give Rhogam and the documentation is inconsistently recorded in 2 charts (EMR and paper). This process results in unnecessary motion (1881 ft.), 45 min. of wasted time searching for information, (10%) potential for missed or duplicate doses, and ultimately not knowing if or when our patients receive Rhogam appropriately.

Once team members agree on the problem or opportunity statement, they move into gap analysis between the current and target states, identify the root cause of the gap, and look for alternative ways to address the problem or opportunity. Jumping to solutions is discouraged.[23] Only when the most promising countermeasure is chosen from several is the team ready to begin the *plan* phase, to design an experiment to test the chosen countermeasure, and to decide who will accomplish each task involved.

Under the *do* section on the A3, we note the experiments and the expected results of those experiments. We often include notes on how the team might adjust the countermeasures if the outcome of the experiment does not meet the goal.

*Study* details our planned and actual results. If the actual results are not what we planned, here is where we ask *why* and—quite often—where we decide we need to rethink the countermeasures or what we are measuring and what we identified as the root cause. If we are not meeting planned results, it is time to adjust our assumptions or our plan.

*Act/Adjust/Standardize.* If the team makes an improvement, a piece of standard work, either changed or created, is a likely result. The team then writes the new standard, updates training, and plans how to spread the new standard. When the team is finished, the people who use the standard work need to demonstrate competency in performing to standard (as noted in chapter 6). This last point is critical to sustainment, so every team is reminded of one of our cardinal rules: an email blast

---

23. Beware of the "backward A3." This is a common trap that leaders or teams will fall into, in which they begin with the solution—because they have already figured it out—and work backward to create the problem statement. This almost always leads to bad analysis and tortured logic.

describing a new standard does not constitute training. We must observe the learner performing to the standard.[24]

The A3 is important in telling the story and also in creating the history of countermeasures and adjustments. We revisit the A3—just like we revisit New Improvement Opportunity slips—over time to assure sustainment. When drift occurs or the environment requires change in the standard, it is always helpful to revisit and update the A3 as we improve the standard. And in Mike Vela's case, having that A3 on hand meant his team could review it along with the standard work and then move through the series of steps described in the standard work in order to respond to the crisis.

Another way to describe problem solving at ThedaCare is that PDSA is our core scientific thinking and the A3 is a kind of Japanese box that surrounds it, with interlocking tools and methods that can be opened like a puzzle box. We often use the term PDSA at ThedaCare, even when we are referring to a full A3. Every organization needs to find the most comfortable language that will be best understood by the people who use it.

Because problem solving is the foundation of the business performance system, every supervisor, manager, and executive entering our leadership training first takes a two-day PDSA course. This course prepares everyone to create and maintain A3s, since every driver on every area improvement board must have a current A3.

We want PDSA to be instilled as a way of thinking about problems. But I should note that we are not strict about A3 documentation. In general, every problem with more than four or five steps (e.g., a phone call, maintenance request, follow-up meeting) and a few possible countermeasures needs a written A3. Even without an A3, we still want PDSA thinking.

---

24.  A sample of a completed A3 is available in the appendix, figure 9.

But if the countermeasure is simple, we are not bureaucratic. For instance, the issue of where to place those surgical gloves in identical operating rooms from chapter 5 did not have a written A3 because a team defined the problem, saw an obvious solution, agreed on it, and ran the experimental glove placement very quickly. The team did fill out a quarter-page New Improvement Opportunity slip for the record, but the additional tools and documentation of an A3 were unnecessary.

Insisting on detailed documentation for every improvement can kill the spirit of innovative problem solving. Similarly, seeking the perfect, complete solution for a problem can kill the urge to experiment and seek new answers. In fact, while we talk about seeking solutions and problem solving, "solved" is a tricky word in the lean world. PDSA is not so much a straight path to the completed solution as it is an endless, forward-moving loop of problem identification, root-cause analysis, hypotheses development, countermeasures, experiments, results tracking, and circling back to check progress. Instead of absolute solutions, we are looking for the best countermeasures, the brilliant *poke yoke*[25] when possible, while we travel toward the solution.

The solution, like the goal, is an ideal state. It is perfection. And the sad truth is we usually do not even know what it looks like or how to get there. All we can do is create targets and aim for them, hoping that each target will become a milestone toward the goal.

Consider the history of influenza immunization, for example. The goal of medical scientists is to eradicate all harmful strains of influenza, but we are not sure how to do this yet. So we create interim targets in order to attack the problem and create measurable outcomes. One target toward reducing annual influenza mortality rates is to get everyone immunized.

---

25. "Poke yoke" means "mistake proofing" in Japanese and refers to methods or devices that prevent or correct errors at the point of creation. In a hospital, this might mean placing an operational button for an x-ray machine behind a lead curtain so the technician is forced to operate at a safe remove.

But this is impractical. Every year, a certain percentage of the population refuses the shot or the shot does not work correctly for a few individuals. We have never been able to immunize everyone, but we have to keep trying. If we target 100% participation, we might have an interim target of 80% immunization rate this year and an 85% target next year while we continue to search out ways to overcome the last stubborn 15% or 5%. So our target of 80% immunization is a stepping-stone toward a 100% immunization goal. We are always a few steps further back than we would like, but at least we are working through the problems and measuring our progress.

Another goal is zero postsurgical infections, year after year. But there are hygiene and diet interactions that we do not yet understand, and there are things in the environment that we cannot yet control—particularly once patients arrive home. So we target improvement over last year's surgical infection rate and keep hoping to glimpse perfection up ahead. Our common stretch target is to double the good and halve the bad with every A3 we write.

If doubling the good and halving the bad were our only targets, we might assign improvement projects to individuals and cut down dramatically on meetings. But our true goal is to create an organization where every person is a problem solver, working the scientific method to fix issues as they arise. We work through problems in teams in order to benefit from many points of view and also to teach PDSA by example. We want this to be the way everyone thinks about and resolves problems, so the scientific method becomes the reflex of clinicians and administrators alike.

In our hospitals, we consider problem solving to be a team sport, and we have found several benefits to working through A3s as a group:

- *Agreement.* Clearly stating a problem is always the first business of a team, and here is where multiple points of view allow us to fully explore the background and current conditions so we can drill down into the issue and define what the problem is and is not. A project about reducing needle sticks can easily become an examination of the weekend staffing mix in the E.D., once a team seeking agreement on the true problem examines the initial data. In fact, I would estimate that teams find we were initially measuring the wrong thing for the problem at hand in half the cases. The need to arrive at consensus teaches us about the problem. Also, countermeasures and standard work that is developed with everyone's participation are more likely to be fairly tested and applied than anything done by a lone hero.

- *A Broad Platform.* With multiple people from different backgrounds on a team, we get broad expertise and experience addressing issues, as well as different ways to look at segmenting data and viewing process flow. Teams learn quickly that many voices make for more robust experiments.

- *Peer Power.* People new to a team experience the pleasure of having peers listen to their ideas, even as they learn the value of the scientific method in everyday problem solving. Together, team members will come up with a better countermeasure than any one of them could alone. Also, learning and practicing PDSA together mean that everyone comes away with the common language of problem solving to use in the future.

Karen Flom has a great illustration of the strength of team problem solving. Self-effacing and fast-talking, Karen is the manager of radiation oncology for the hospitals and is accustomed to dealing with evolving therapies and technology. That does not mean, however, that it is easy to incorporate new machines and technology into a busy department.

"When I first joined the unit in 2007, the business performance system was not in place, and we were in the process of adding a cutting-edge treatment machine, Cyberknife, that delivers radiation from 360 degrees around the tumor. As I remember it, the directive was that we could 'probably' add this new technology without adding staff," Karen says. The Cyberknife manufacturer, meanwhile, strongly recommended that we hire five additional staff members—radiation therapists, physicists, and a program coordinator—to handle the technology and patient flow.

"It was true that not all of our treatment machines were running at full capacity," Karen says. "So I came up with a plan. I made assumptions about how we could block out treatment time for the different therapies. With the unit supervisor, I looked at the data and figured out how it would all work."

"Then I laid out the plan for our two lead radiation therapists. They kept shaking their heads and saying, 'I don't think so. I don't think that's going to work,'" Karen remembers. "I thought my job was to convince them. I told them, 'Look, you guys; I have the data.' They could not tell me they were at full capacity. There were holes in the schedule where we did not have patients but we still had staff. Based on the annual data, I was sure we could just reblock the schedule and make it work. So I wasn't truly listening to them because my focus was delivering a plan that met financial performance. That meant doing it without adding staff."

It was not until after the Cyberknife was installed and launched that it became apparent the lead radiation therapists had been right. Patients did not arrive when or in the order that Karen predicted. There was too much scrambling, and some patient needs were not being met. ThedaCare was still early in its lean journey at this point, but Karen and her supervisor pulled together a kaizen team to reconsider work flow and scheduling. In the end, she had to hire and train two new radiation therapists in the hectic process instead of having everyone trained and ready at launch. It was a valuable lesson of what can happen when relevant voices are not heard.

Three years later, we were preparing to add another exciting new technology to the menu: high-dose rate brachytherapy. Small and nimble, HDR brachy did not need to be fixed in a dedicated vault of its own like other radiation therapies. We could save money by colocating the HDR brachy inside one of the lead-lined vaults used for the external-beam radiation machines. It was a solution that presented its own logistical issues, and Karen almost had a flashback to the previous near disaster. In the intervening years, however, her unit had been trained to problem solve as a team and was operating under the business performance system. They knew to start an A3 for new initiatives and opportunities, as well as for traditional problems.

"When I told the team we were getting the HDR brachy, two clinical leads stepped forward and asked if they could own the project," Karen says. "They designed the space and the staffing flow. They ran mock trials, wrote standard work, and tweaked the process. They ran experiments and collected data and used it to drive decisions. They completed cross-training and kept everyone up-to-date during our team huddles."

Karen's job was to mentor the team and coordinate with other departments when needed. By the time the machine arrived, everyone on the unit had been involved in experiments around the design of the space and the work flow, so nothing was a surprise.

"For me, the one thing that really defines the difference between the old world and the new is this: in the past, we used data to prove a point, to bolster an argument. Now, we use data to make decisions, and that has made a huge change," Karen says. "A team using data as a guide will be smarter every time than a single person trying to prove a solution."

Karen used to have to tell people she could not fix their problems. These days, she helps people who are on their way to solving issues themselves. And Mike Vela gets home in time to play with his children and to Barbecue when the weather is nice.

As long as we can see the problem, we have the confidence and the structure in place to address it. But what about the complications we cannot see clearly? This is where making problems visual and tracking them becomes a critical need. Let's move on to transparency.

Chapter **8**

# Transparency/Visual
## Management

Of all the issues that lurk in our hospital corridors, patient satisfaction can be the most difficult to see and therefore address.
Composed partly of the care we offer and partly of the care
that people want and expect, satisfaction seems unique to each patient.
Beyond the need to feel better, patients also need the emotional connection of true sympathy and attention—unless they really just need to
be left alone. They want good food with real flavor, but everyone hates
at least one vegetable, and nobody wants painful therapies, even if they
are sometimes necessary.

Meanwhile, surveys such as the Hospital Consumer Assessment of
Healthcare Providers and Systems, or HCAHPS, are becoming pivotal
to our survival.[26] Now that federal rules attach Medicare compensation
to performance on the HCAHPS Survey, satisfaction is affecting our

---

26. The HCAHPS Survey, developed by CMS and the federal Agency for Healthcare Research
and Quality, is a 32-question survey measuring patients' perceptions of their recent hospital
experiences. In use since 2002, HCAHPS is the first survey of common metrics in use
across the nation. And there are consequences to poor performance. CMS has set threshold
targets for healthcare organizations to achieve in patient satisfaction and has begun lowering
reimbursement for those who fail.

bottom line. Yet, it seemed impossible to move the needle on our overall patient satisfaction scores until we pushed the issue out into the open and made it visible. Satisfaction scoring is one potent area in which transparency and visual management can make all the difference, so let's use our work there to illustrate.

We began our investigation into patient satisfaction, as usual, by trying to define the root. What is satisfaction? The effectiveness of our therapies should be the main component of the definition, but we knew that satisfaction in healthcare is powerfully shaped by an array of hidden issues, conditions, expectations, and personal tastes that make it very difficult for hospitals to score well on standardized patient surveys. Still, we had to begin somewhere.

When hospital leaders began looking into improving our federal HCAHPS scores in 2012, we settled upon a hypothesis that nurse-patient communication was a key component to satisfaction. This, we decided, was the virtual lever behind most of the HCAHPS questions. Examples of survey questions include: *Did the nurses treat you with courtesy and respect? How often did nurses carefully listen to you?* Other questions are subtler but still speak to the nurse-patient relationship: *Did you get help getting to the bathroom as soon as you wanted? How well was your pain controlled?*

We needed a way to standardize nursing communication so that we could perform experiments and improve it. This sounds like a tall order, but we have a trusted process to follow, and that makes all the difference. We created a cross-functional team that wrote an A3 stating our intention to improve HCAHPS by focusing on nursing communications. Our experiments involved creating a series of questions nurses would ask every patient every hour (or every two hours at night, depending on patient condition and wakefulness).

The team decided on six key items for nurses to touch upon during these bedside visits, which we called Purposeful Patient Visits. And because we like alliteration, we identified the six items as pain, positioning, potty, possessions (everything in reach), patient specifics (safety, individual treatments such as ice packs or breathing tubes), and pump (IV). A Purposeful Patient Visit went like this:

"Hello, Mr. Smith. Can you tell me your pain level right now? Are you comfortable in that position? Do you need to use the bathroom or bedpan? Do you have everything you need? How about your book or the television remote? I see that you're scheduled for an x-ray today. That should happen within the next hour. I see your IV fluids need to be changed. I'll do that now. I will be back in an hour to check on you or another nurse will in my place."

By now, it is a ThedaCare reflex to think about ways to make visual our efforts, data, and experiments. So, outside every patient door we attached a chart with the six Ps and a timetable for a nurse to initial for every hour's visit. Every time a visit did not happen, the reason was noted. Those reasons were then collected on Pareto charts for the unit, which were displayed on the unit's area improvement center along with an action plan to address the reasons that visits did not occur. Metrics from every unit were then pulled together into a weekly report that was displayed on my improvement board outside my office door.

Our immediate goal was saturation. We wanted every single nurse to be 100% competent on the Purposeful Patient Visit dialogue after six visits that were observed for competence, usually by a clinical lead or nursing supervisor. We wanted every unit where these visits[27] were implemented to be doing it correctly 90% of the time within three months. This required teamwork on the units to ensure that every patient was

---

27. Nurses in units with one-to-one care, such as the ICU, or a Family Birth Center, where care is structured differently, do not use Purposeful Patient Visits.

seen every hour during the day. And we got there. All medical and surgical units were reporting at least 90% compliance on Purposeful Patient Visits within three months.

Three months later, when we had our first HCAHPS scores that could be compared to our fully realized Purposeful Patient Visits, we had a little surprise. The numbers were going the wrong way. In late 2013, after three full months of data, the team had to admit that HCAHPS scores were not being affected by our Purposeful Patient Visits. So the team returned to the study/adjust phase of the A3 cycle and began root-cause analysis anew. Our early hypothesis was that patient experiences in the E.D.—where nurses were not practicing purposeful visits because of incompatible work flow—have a larger impact on HCAHPS scores than we anticipated. Testing of this hypothesis has been launched with results still to be determined.

I tell you this uncomfortable fact in order to underline the importance of adjusting expectations. Success is rarely immediate or quick. Big, complex questions such as improving patient satisfaction are not usually "solved" in the first experiment. Experiments, by definition, are not always successful. In fact, if failure is impossible, you are conducting an invalid experiment. It is crucial, therefore, that everyone appreciates what they can learn from failures as well as what can be gleaned from success.

For me, the lesson I would share from this experiment is not the result. It is this: the power of visual management is such that, in the space of three months while using simple posted checklists and charts, we changed and standardized the way nurses communicate with patients in all of our medical and surgical units. We spread a new piece of standard work—requiring a big time commitment and new work habits—and achieved better than 90% adoption.

Visual management ensured that nurses were reminded at every patient door and at every daily huddle of the daily communication schedule and the standardized content of that communication. Unit nurses worked together in teams to make sure all patient visits were covered and that reasons were noted on every chart when a visit was skipped. And nurses reported seeing a positive change in their patient relationships even if it did not show up on HCAHPS scores. They established a level of immediate trust by promising a return visit in one hour—and then following up—and by proactively meeting patient needs instead of scrambling after call lights.[28] Even if those visits did not move the needle on HCAHPS, nurses saw the positive change and so adopted the work methods as their own.

Despite its demonstrated effectiveness for spurring improvement, transparency and visual management can be difficult for some hospitals to imagine. These are public displays of defects, after all. In the business world, transparency and sharing data are often described as "opening the kimono," and that kind of openness can feel uncomfortable. Do we really want family members to know that we are reminding nurses to check on patient welfare every hour? What if patients read our huddle boards and see our errors and defects?

Here is what I have learned, having been a leader in both transparent and opaque systems: patients and family know our faults and trouble spots already. Our defects are not news to them. What huddle boards and area improvement centers communicate is that we are using the scientific method to try to solve those problems. Visual management and transparency tell the story of our efforts to improve.

---

28. While we have not done the necessary work to establish direct relationship, we have noticed that incidence of patient call lights and patient falls decreased markedly when PPVs were introduced. We hypothesize that patient falls decreased as a result of patient confidence that a nurse would return at a specific time to assist movement.

Visual management is a promise. Like a wedding ring on your finger for everyone to see, you are stating your commitment to improved patient outcomes. And patients notice. When they talk to us about those Purposeful Patient Visit check sheets or the charts that depict our experiments to address infection rates post-Caesarian section, they are consistently positive, even grateful, that we have noticed the defects that they know about already.

A word of caution, however: huddle boards will also reveal a lack of discipline and care if the measures and data are not kept fresh. Imagine being taken for a walk on your brand-new knee down an orthopedics surgery hallway to come across a board showing postsurgical infection rates. Pausing to rest, you notice that the data have not been updated for a month. This would make anyone question the unit's commitment to solving problems. Are the nurses and doctors paying attention to infection? Once we start telling patients the full truth, we cannot stop.

Keeping metrics and data fresh is critical for the unit employees, as well. Nobody wants to do extra work if the results are not important enough to post and keep current. But we do like knowing what happens next. We want to be able to look at a board and follow the continuing story of a problem, the experiments attempted, and how it is being resolved. Having daily huddles around the board, assigning team members to "own" certain metrics, and reviewing the material constantly help keep our data fresh.

In our hospitals, we also encourage snooping. We want nurses, leads, managers, and physicians to go and check out the area improvement centers and huddle boards on other units. And we celebrate those boards that can tell a story clearly and quickly. The benefit is cross-germination of ideas throughout the hospitals.

For instance, our two emergency departments had been under pressure to reduce personnel hours. Emergency services is a notoriously difficult department to staff since fluctuations in patient need can be striking and nobody schedules an emergency visit in advance. Yet, we never want to be caught understaffed in the face of a crisis, so we are often overstaffed out of caution. For weeks, the E.D. huddles at Theda Clark and Appleton Medical Center struggled with new ideas and experiments in reducing staff hours, noted trends on their huddle boards, and tried to find new ways to forecast need. It was slow work.

Then, MaryJeanne Schaffmeyer noticed that the huddle board at Theda Clark's E.D. started showing a real decline in staff hours worked, week over week, at the same volume of patients. She read the story, asked a few questions, and walked away excited.

"So, I go and nudge the folks over at AMC's emergency department. I tell them they should take a look at what Theda Clark is doing. It's really cool," MaryJeanne says. "They don't exactly shrug, but they don't jump on it, either. So I try again—nudge, nudge."

Finally, MaryJeanne called a meeting, knowing that a little transparency goes a long way. She had both departments show their results on the project to reduce hours, and all that green on Theda Clark's charts got AMC's attention.

MaryJeanne explains: "Here's what Theda Clark was doing. They noticed the natural rhythms on day shift: plenty of patients first thing and usually tapering off by early afternoon. So they started having a quick meeting in the early afternoon every day. On slow days, the manager or supervisor would say, 'OK, anybody want a few hours off?' If anyone did, they could clock out. It was completely voluntary."

There were enough days that had two or three or five working hours removed, so it made a real difference in the staff costs for the week.

Nobody was making a new schedule or new rules; people were being flexible and communicating with each other. As a result, the nurses in emergency often had the opportunity to grab a couple extra hours of free time in the afternoon—a gift both *from* and *to* their colleagues.

Soon after, AMC's emergency department adopted the same approach. After a month of those afternoon "needs" meetings, the E.D. had managed to reduce its staff-hours-worked metric by 3.1%.

We encourage leaders to study one another's boards, to shamelessly steal any idea that appeals. The labor and delivery units, for instance, have some of the same staffing issues that we see in emergency because babies are terrible at announcing their birth schedules in advance. Those units have begun experimenting with the same needs-scheduling meetings.

Transparency helps us create a common language, a shared understanding of how ideas and experiments play out, how trend lines get pushed. The huddle boards, kamishibai, and area improvement centers become the bones of the system—a visual aid like those hanging skeletons that doctors used to use to illustrate how things worked deep inside the body.

All of this openness does have a few hazards, of course. Leaders can become accustomed to standing in front of boards or walking through gemba, chatting about conditions around us and forgetting about people's perceptions and power rankings within the organization. One morning, for instance, I got off the elevator at the ICU and noticed an award sitting on a small table, noting that our hospital was number one in successful organ donations in the state of Wisconsin. A great achievement, to be sure, but I paused a step wondering whether that should be lying around in the ICU. A few more feet down the hallway, I saw the huddle board with a large poster, again congratulating everyone on being tops in organ donations.

I turned to the lead nurse standing nearby and said, "I wonder how patients feel about that." She blanched. Later, I heard that she was upset at being personally critiqued by the president of hospitals, and I felt terrible because I am very proud of this team and their accomplishments. I simply forgot how much weight my words can carry.

While it is true that there is something a bit unfeeling about trumpeting our success in providing organs from the ICU, where so many cling perilously to life, I should have simply congratulated the nurse on this distinction and then asked her manager if that poster might cause problems with patients or family members. I should have said, "Ask your team about perceptions from a family's point of view, and then, if there is a problem, maybe you can discuss countermeasures such as moving the poster out of the public eye." It is important that we remember to consider how people will feel about comments from "the big boss" while encouraging everyone from surgeons to administrative assistants to think creatively and openly about solving problems.

Transparency should create an environment where we are always questioning, looking for alternatives, and finding new paths. Those questions, asked in an open and supportive environment, then become teaching and mentoring opportunities as well as prospects for deeper investigations.

And sometimes, putting our troubles and defects on display shows how our work is connected across a complex organization. Shana Herzfeldt told me a story about this that stuck with me. Now a director of operations, Shana is an RN and one of the architects of our Collaborative Care[29]

---

29. A revolutionary change in how we care for people on inpatient units, Collaborative Care was developed as part of ThedaCare's early lean transformation. This model helped us leap ahead on quality, such as eliminating medication reconciliation errors, while reducing costs. Every unit in our hospitals has been redesigned to this model, which we have also shared with other lean healthcare organizations.

method of operations. One of the core tenants of Collaborative Care is that all patients and their families will be seen by a full care team—doctor, nurse, pharmacist, and care manager—within 90 minutes of admittance to a hospital unit to develop a complete care plan.

Shana was looking at the huddle board for the hospitalists when she noticed a New Improvement Opportunity Slip that sounded familiar.[30] There was too much variation in the amount of time it took to get an emergency patient moved from the E.D. to the unit where a bed was waiting, the slip's author noted. The hospital unit would be alerted that a patient was coming, the Collaborative Care team would be called, and then it might be five minutes or two hours before the patient actually arrived. This was causing lost time and aggravation for inpatient care teams.

The problem sounded familiar because Shana had seen it on a nursing manager's board, she realized. Since the teams were all interconnected, she realized that it would probably show up soon enough on a pharmacy huddle board, as well. After coordinating with the different groups, Shana pulled together a cross-functional kaizen team. They wrote an A3 that defined the problem, set the scope, and created a goal: patients should get from the E.D. to the medical floor within 40 minutes of the admission decision 80% of the time. (In the current state, patients arrived within 40 minutes just 28% of the time.) Those 40 minutes were often necessary for patient stabilization, surgical consultations, and other preparations for moving an emergency case to the unit. Any time beyond 40 minutes was considered a defect in making the handoff.

Shana and her team quickly discovered that folks in the E.D. were just as frustrated with the handoff process and happy to help out. The team, now including representatives of the E.D., mapped the current state of

---

30. An example of a New Improvement Opportunity slip is available in the appendix, figure 7.

the handoff, created an ideal state, and then made a plan for closing the gap. During the investigation, the team realized that they could improve the hospital's financial picture while they were at it, since we were relying on two full-time nurses to act as hospital access supervisors (like air traffic controllers). What we really needed was one reliable, repeatable process. The team conducted trials; found a process that got them to their 40-minute goal 80% of the time; and then wrote, trained, and observed the new standard work for the handoff.

This is what I mean about speaking the same language, sharing ideas, and making our ideas and defects transparent. A visual workplace creates its own kind of momentum toward change because good people cannot look at a clearly stated problem every day without wanting to fix it. They just need the tools, the time, and our permission to do so.

Having outside expertise to help fill in the gaps created by our individual backgrounds and education is also incredibly helpful. This is why we push for cross-functional teams and why we created advisory teams to assist every manager, as you will see in the next chapter.

# Chapter 9

# Advisory
## Teams

Most ThedaCare managers begin their careers as excellent clinicians. They are nurses, therapists, or pharmacists who impress everyone with the way they take personal responsibility for their work, who prove they can move obstacles and get things done for their patients. As a reward, we ask them to be fully accountable for the finances and operational management of the small business that is their unit or clinic.

We know that reward-by-promotion can stress our most valuable people when there is little or no preparation offered for the leap from clinical practice to management. The question we confronted in 2008 as we were developing the business performance system was how to help managers acquire skills for their new responsibilities. We did not want them to drop what they were doing and get advanced degrees in business administration. What we really wanted was for them to magically have all the skills they needed and the time to focus on improvement work. We lacked the right wand, however.

Our first experiments in helping managers focus on improvement ended poorly. These were our "circuit riding" experiments, mentioned earlier, in which a lean facilitator would come to a unit, teach the manager how to write an A3, set up data collection, and create the area improvement board. Then the facilitator would ride off, expecting the manager to maintain the projects and practices. Soon enough, however, another priority would percolate to the surface, a larger fire would break out demanding the manager's attention, and improvement projects would languish on the boards.

Reviewing the results of those first experiments, our business performance system focus group realized two things: managers should not alone bear the burden and excitement of big improvement projects and we were still operating as if we were stuck in silos.

In those days before the business performance system, people identified strongly with their silo. Either you were operations (the front line) working in one of the many clinical units or you were support services. Within support, there were many silos or departments: quality, finance, education, marketing, human resources, security, and facilities. And each of those support services had an agenda to press on our operations managers. So, finance might meet with a manager to discuss unit performance and then present budget targets for the coming year. Quality team members might come in with charts showing that the unit was not hitting a new organizational target for infection rates or patient falls and then talk about what the manager might do to improve her numbers. Next, educators might drop by and announce that new training needed to be scheduled, while human resources wanted to talk about improving employee morale. Meanwhile, the manager would be struggling to keep up.

What we needed was to put everyone on the same team, in service to the patients. Our focus group started talking about how to shift the dynamic so that everyone from every silo was supporting improvement at the front line. We came up with the idea of an advisory team for each manager that might look like an idealized board of directors, a group of experts from different fields who came together to support the frontline unit.

Because we were trying to take stress off the managers, we did not want this to be a passive advisory panel, unengaged in the work of improvement, or a contentious group meeting once a quarter to pass judgment on the leader's performance. We wanted a group that would share the manager's burden.

Therefore, we decided that members of the cross-functional advisory team would "own" the unit's major improvement initiatives that we call drivers. And membership on the advisory teams would be as dynamic over time as the unit's changing needs.

To illustrate, let's look at the Family Birth Center at Appleton Medical Center, where Debra VandenLangenberg (everyone calls her Deb V.) is the manager. Like most managers, Deb's area improvement board usually has six or eight main drivers related to safety, quality, customer satisfaction, people, and financial stewardship. Her advisory board is composed of the unit supervisor, one of the clinical leads, an educator,[31] a quality analyst, a newborn specialist,[32] a financial analyst, and a lean facilitator. In addition, Deb's roster of ad hoc advisors who might join the team as their specialized knowledge is needed includes representatives of ThedaCare's marketing, security, materials management, facilities, and decision resources departments.[33] A set of fresh eyes from outside the area is also included to question everyone's assumptions.

---

31. An educator is usually an RN who works for our education department, teaching and organizing ongoing clinical training as well as spreading best practices.

32. This is a nurse from the Family Birth Center who acts as a specialist in treatment and care of newborn babies.

33. This department produces and helps us pull the data that guides our decisions.

Deb's fresh eyes belong to a manager from a local CVS pharmacy who was interested in learning more about lean.

The advisory team roster can include a lot of people. But who owns the improvement work? On Deb's team, it is the Birth Center's supervisor, a clinical lead, the newborn specialist, and a quality analyst. They are in charge of collecting and updating the data on their own particular drivers. The metric owner also helps move the work along by checking on progress throughout the month. Deb explained that her direct reports typically own most or all of the unit's main drivers because they, the unit team members, are most interested in the outcomes. If there is a big push on a particular project out of the quality department, however, the quality analyst might own that driver. The analyst still reports to his or her boss in the quality department during this time but is responsible to the team and Deb for moving the project forward. It is a very flexible system, and Deb, like most managers, encourages her advisory team members to take the lead on projects to which they are drawn.

These were Deb's 2012 advisory team roster and drivers:[34]

---

34.  Our standard work for creating an advisory team is available in the appendix, figure 10.

| Name | Role | | Drivers Owned | | | |
|---|---|---|---|---|---|---|
| | | | 2010 | 2011 | 2012 | 2013 |
| Deb VandenLangenberg | Manager | 2010–present | Productivity | Productivity | Productivity | Productivity |
| | | | Managed Expenses | Managed Expenses | | On Call |
| | | | | | | Force Overs |
| Lisa Reed | Supervisor | 2010–present | Medication Near Miss | Lactation Output Services | Surgical Counts | Reconciled Controlled Substances |
| Jessica Van Lannen | Educator | 2012–present | | | Tdap Administration | |
| Stacy Carson | Lead RN | 2010–present | Pain Documentation | Medication Near Miss | Pain Documentation | Purposeful Patient Visit |
| Sharon Morgan | Quality | 2010–May 2013 | Perinatal Vacuum Bundle | < 39 Week Elective Delivery | < 39 Week Elective Delivery | 3 & 4th Degree Lacerations |
| Sara Bronson | Quality | April 2013–present | | | | NTVD Bundle |
| | | | | | | 3 & 4th Degree Lacerations |
| Mary Jo Biedermann | Newborn Specialist | 2012–present | | | Newborn pain documentation | Mock or Code NRP Attendance |
| Jill Pierret | Financial Analyst | 2010–present | | | | |
| Patsy Engel | TIS Facilitator | 2010–2011 | | | | |

| Ad Hoc Members | Role |
|---|---|
| Julie Martin | Manager - CVS Fresh eyes |
| Susan Dietrich | HR |
| Angelia Squires | Decision Resources |
| Pam Kitzinger | Material Management |
| Beth Stubing | Coordinator of Community Services |
| Amy Lotzer | Marketing |
| Varying OB Providers | Clinical |
| Mike Powell | Security |
| Cliff Schneider | Facilities |

Deb's 2012 Advisory Team Roster and Drivers

The productivity metric for the Family Birth Center is the same as every other unit in that we are always looking for 3.1% annual improvement. Lisa's driver and her project to improve it involved accounting for all leftover surgical items to ensure none remained in the patient. Jessica was working toward improved rates of Tdap immunizations (for tetanus, diphtheria, and acellular pertussis, better known as whooping cough). Stacey's metric involved better documentation of patient pain levels by nurses. Sharon was working to reduce the number of patients electing to induce labor prior to the thirty-ninth week of pregnancy, and Mary Jo was improving the frequency in which nurses assessed and recorded pain levels in newborn babies.

Once the target on a driver has been achieved and the improved process appears stable, the team can move the project from the "drivers" to a "watch" list. During a year, a unit such as Deb's might have six drivers or 10, depending on how quickly they meet their targets.

What roles are played by advisory team members who do not own drivers, such as Jill Pierret and Patsy Engel? As a ThedaCare financial analyst, Jill was there to help Deb—who had been an excellent nurse but was never an accountant or business analyst—to think about her unit's finances and use a general ledger. Patsy, a lean facilitator, was there to help the team choose and use lean tools when developing A3s and designing experiments. And analysts such as Sharon, who are versed in issues and advancements affecting healthcare quality around the nation and world, helped Deb stay on top of the most current thinking.

The advisory team generally meets once a month, using a standardized meeting format. Everyone who owns a driver offers a five-minute update, and then the team shares ideas on how to move work forward. For me, this is the most exciting meeting of the month. The energy that comes from a room of people talking about improvement ideas and root causes and countermeasures is infectious.

"The real advantage to this system is the connections that we've made between clinical units and support departments," Deb says. "We've broken down those silos, and we're all working together."

While we set up the system to help managers in operations, we found that the business performance system works equally well in support functions. Departments overseeing quality and finance, for instance, employ daily huddles, advisory teams, and scorecards to help advance their own improvement work and to spread new methods across the various units where members are working. Daily stat sheets are not always useful in support departments where the work flow is much different from that in hospital units, but managers are working on ways to bring those daily conversations with frontline workers into their standard work.

So far, though, the biggest change advisory teams have brought to our hospitals is a growing cohesion among medical units, support functions, and specialty groups such as surgery or the cardiac catheterization lab, which often send representatives to join advisory teams in order to improve transitions of care and patient flow. Like we hoped, we are shifting from internally focused silos to a more unified hospital, focused on the patient.

"Being on teams now, I understand the work a whole lot better, beyond the metrics and data," says Gina Moon, Jill Pierret's boss and director of finance operations. "When you are sitting at a desk back here [in a support office], it's hard to know what they are dealing with on the floor."

The conversation that someone such as Gina might have with Deb has broadened considerably. Before 2009, talk was limited to budgets and variances in the P&L[35] statements, Gina says. Finance would give managers targets and then talk about why the managers were not hitting those targets. They were not dynamic meetings, filled with ideas.

---

35. Profit and loss statements.

"But recently, I was working with the manager of a medical-surgery unit whose productivity numbers were suddenly going the wrong way," Gina says. "Surgeries were down, labor was up, and they still felt just as busy as ever."

Now that Gina was on the manager's advisory team and not just an analyst wielding a P&L, they got together and thought about how to find the root cause of the problem and started with a simple calendar. For every day of the week, they wrote down the surgeries performed and the labor hours on the unit. Thursday suddenly stuck out like a sore thumb.

On Thursdays, blocks of time were being reserved in the O.R. but were not being used by the provider who asked for it. These were small blocks scattered throughout the day but predominantly on Thursdays. The staffing was the same as Wednesday and Friday, but O.R. revenue was definitely reduced on Thursdays.

"Using that simple calendar, we discovered that in order to get productivity numbers back under control, she had to work with providers on how they were scheduling time in the O.R. She thought the problem was her staffing mix, but it was something else entirely," Gina says.

"We used to spend a lot of time and energy on budgets. What we produced was always wrong, but that is most of what we talked about," Gina says. "I don't really talk financial terms to managers anymore. I talk about improvement metrics and productivity. This is a partnership now; I'm part of a team."

Back when we first implemented the business performance system and I was still a vice president, I attended as many advisory team meetings as I could. I wanted to assess how the experiment was going, and I really liked the energy in those meetings. One of my clearest memories is of being in an advisory team meeting in an oncology unit, where the metric for their safety driver focused on patient falls. The work was successful, the processes to avoid falls were stable, and the team, frankly, was getting anxious to move on. There had not been a single patient fall in a year. Yet there had been three central (IV) line infections in the past several months.

There was a brief update on the safety driver, and then I remember the team's educator turning to me and saying, "Kim, we were hoping it would be all right with you if we moved patient falls to the watch list and moved on to look at preventing those infections."

If memory serves, I said, "Thank you for asking and I hope you don't feel like you ever have to ask permission again. Absolutely! Move on to the next problem."

Nobody asks for permission anymore, largely because we have learned to make the question "Is it time to move on?" part of our discussion around every driver. We also make sure to talk about what the next projects might be. We do not want one driver to linger just because we are not sure about the next most critical thing.

As president of the hospitals, I have an advisory team, too, which includes all three vice presidents, directors of quality and finance, and other executives. Our drivers are a bit broader than those at the unit level. Currently, these drivers include:

- Safety: Drug diversions

- Quality: Preventable mortality[36] and 30-day hospital readmissions

- People: HCAHPS scores and using force overs[37] to manage capacity

- Financial Stewardship: 3.1% productivity improvement

---

36. We are focused more specifically now on eliminating cases of sepsis.

37. A force over is a mandatory lengthening of a nurse's shift in order to meet demand.

The drivers on the area improvement board outside my office door remain somewhat broad because all of the unit drivers roll up onto mine. So Deb's surgical-counts driver results land in my quality lane. After all, any surgical equipment left in a patient certainly adds to my 30-day-readmission driver. At times there are unit-level drivers that do not match up cleanly to the True North, but that is considered acceptable as long as the work benefits patients.

Along with stat sheets and huddles, these advisory teams have been the biggest levers we have to help our managers move from firefighting to leading. On the day that I talked to Deb about her experiences with her team, she was still recovering from a very big day on her unit. Two of her top deputies were on vacation and, as will happen, it seemed as though every pregnant woman in a 50-mile radius chose that day to deliver.

Deb reminisced about 2008, when she was interim manager and every day felt like a series of emergencies and she had only the spare moment to catch up and learn new skills, such as how to change the direction of her P&L. But on this day, when it really was an urgent situation, Deb enjoyed the chance to spend a couple of hours in the clinical lead position, making sure everyone's needs were covered.

"At this point, I get to spend a lot of time with the huddle board and advisory team, dreaming up the next big improvement," Deb says. "It's so rare that I am needed on the floor it was actually a pleasure."

Advisory teams have done a great job of level loading the work of managers and of breaking down silos between operations, support, and specialty areas. But how do we *know* that advisory teams—or any other element of the business performance system—are actually moving the needle on our improvement goals? Let's move on to the way we keep ourselves honest and our aim true: the scorecard.

# Chapter 10

# Scorecards

Shawn Chartier knew trucks. He could break down the manufacturing process for concrete mixers, refuse trucks, and fire engines from cab to transfer case. He knew every step in the production sequence and was always looking for the problems that might interrupt flow. But he was not really a truck guy. Shawn was a lean thinker, an engineer who knew how to use and trust data, completely taken with the idea of continuous improvement.

And that is how he came to be gowned and scrubbed up, standing in the middle of an operating room and watching an open-heart surgery just two months after he came to work for ThedaCare.

"My old company was sort of dabbling with lean," Shawn says. "One day, I read about ThedaCare and its commitment to lean, so I got in touch to see if I could take my knowledge further. I was hired as a lean facilitator and then assigned to the open-heart surgery program and the ICU. It was incredible."

Shawn, who still talks about being in that surgical suite with wide-eyed awe, was doing exactly what he had done at Oshkosh Corporation: watching the flow, looking for waste, relying on facts to guide his projects. From people such as Shawn we have learned that lean work in hospitals is not so different from lean in factories. Whether the system is making truck bodies or fixing human bodies, a lean organization succeeds or fails on its ability to create a culture of problem solvers, set organization-wide goals, and honestly assess progress toward those goals.

In our system, we use a scorecard for those honest assessments. Every unit or clinic has one, as do division vice presidents and I. Each scorecard shows the status and progress toward the goal on five to eight major improvement projects, such as reducing hospital readmissions or eliminating drug thefts. Scorecards are reviewed monthly by the scorecard owner and his or her boss—or, as we call a boss, a one-up. They are also the main focus of the monthly advisory-team meeting. Scorecards are tailored to each unit while still reflecting the major goals of the hospital's division and the company as a whole. Nearly every project on a scorecard can be traced directly to ThedaCare's True North and our organizational strategic goals.[38]

The scorecard tells us whether our hard work and best intentions are actually moving the needle and keeps our feet in objective reality. Scorecards are built with verified data, not arguable opinions, so we have a solid platform on which to base our discussions and decisions.

Scorecards also encourage us to take the long view. Stat sheets are a daily tool, helping us to think proactively while looking for potential defects and trends. Huddles are daily tools with a slightly longer-term focus, used to discuss projects, experiments, and countermeasures. The scorecard is

---

38. The business performance system, along with scorecards, began in the hospitals division but has steadily spread throughout the ThedaCare system to divisions such as primary care and hospice.

| Area | Metric | Owner | YTD Results | YTD Target | On/Off Target |
|------|--------|-------|-------------|------------|---------------|
| Safety | DART - AMC | Mark | 1.29 | 1.96 | |
| Safety | DART - TC | Mark | 1.70 | 2.76 | |
| Quality | MRSA Infection Per 1000 Pt Days (AMC/TC ICU) | Mark | 0 | 1.25 | |
| Quality | 30 Day Readmission Rate (AMC and TC) | Mark | 8.50% | 7.90% | ■ |
| Customer | % Top Box - AMC | Jill | 74.30% | 74.61% | ■ |
| Customer | % Top Box - TC | Jill | 72.60% | 69.56% | |
| People | HAT Score - AMC | Jill | 82.24 | 82.58 | ■ |
| People | HAT Score - TC | Jill | 81.99 | 81.97 | |
| Financial | Inf. Gross Rev/Productive Hour - AMC | Mary Jeanne | 6.39% | 3.10% | |
| Financial | Inf. Gross Rev/Productive Hour - TC | Mary Jeanne | 2.79% | 3.10% | ■ |
| Financial | Operating Margin - AMC | Mary Jeanne | 8.04% | 2.00% | |
| Financial | Operating Margin - TC | Mary Jeanne | 7.03% | -0.80% | |

KEY: ▨ GREEN  ■ RED

**True North Summary**

one step removed from the daily noise. This is where we look hard in the mirror and gauge whether we are moving in the right direction. The scorecard facilitates accountability.

So, what improvement activities belong on a scorecard? To answer that, let me break all improvement projects into three types:

- Quick: We can find and deploy a countermeasure in about three steps. It might require a team's general agreement, a phone call, and a maintenance work order. Think of the project in which a surgical team decided to place gloves in the same spot in every operating room. That is a quick project.

- Focused: This improvement requires an A3 and might need more than one experiment to find the right countermeasure, but it can be accomplished entirely on the unit. In chapter 7, for instance, when Mike Vela and his team created standard work for responding to emergency drug shortages, they were doing a focused improvement project.

- Systemic: This project often crosses department lines, affects the standard work of more than one unit or department, and requires collaboration from outside teams. But systemic projects are mostly distinguished by their importance to the goals of the entire organization. An ICU project to measurably tighten controls on drug dispensing, for example, ties directly to our system-wide goal to eliminate drug thefts.

Projects that end up on scorecards are all *systemic* projects because they are important to the goals of the entire institution. Systemic projects are typically designed to move the needle on a scorecard driver, and while its focus narrows and becomes more specific as it filters down to the unit level, it is still of system-wide importance.

For instance, ThedaCare's True North metric for the entire organization in the "quality" category was preventable mortality. The goal was to eliminate it. So, my scorecard for the hospitals contained data on preventable mortality and an A3 detailing root causes and countermeasures.

Meanwhile, the physician group in charge of caring for patients on the medical units—the hospitalists—chose to focus attention on reducing cases of sepsis infection as a way to decrease preventable mortality and increase quality. As is true of any system-sized improvement project, this systemic project was a tall order.

The physician lead of the hospitalist program and medical director of Theda Clark Medical Center, James McGovern, MD, is a careful, deliberate man. Before deciding on a quality project, he sat down with the charts of every patient who died over a two-year period and looked for less than perfect care. The full-body reaction to infection known as sepsis was surprisingly frequent.

In fact, septic shock was a cause in 15%–20% of preventable patient deaths, Dr. McGovern found. This is consistent with national averages but far too high. So, he pulled together a team of fellow doctors, a clinical IT analyst, an educator who had shown interest in improving our sepsis rates, and, of course, fresh eyes. The team created an A3 and identified three major root causes of preventable mortality from septic shock: lack of early identification of sepsis, failure to administer timely antibiotics, and failure to give aggressive volume resuscitation.[39]

The first root cause involved caregivers recognizing combinations of symptoms; the second and third could be effectively countered with standard work. The team saw that everyone on a hospital unit needed to know the best practices for treating septic shock—to have specific

---

39. For patients in septic shock, a best-practice treatment for dangerously low blood pressure is to increase the pressure by flooding the body with extra fluid in order to fill the abnormally enlarged veins and arteries.

instructions in easy reach. But first, we needed to recognize the signs of a full-body inflammatory response early enough to avoid septic shock in our vulnerable patients.

Patients suffering from sepsis often feel terrible. As the infection spreads inflammation throughout the body, patients become feverish; hyperventilation and confusion are common side effects. But each symptom can be related to several other factors; it is the combination of symptoms that alerts clinicians. And patients are sometimes unable to communicate symptoms to anyone. We needed to rely on data as well as patient reports.

The systemic improvement project is still at the early stages as of this writing, but I am excited about the possibilities of one countermeasure that ran as an experiment with patients admitted to one of our hospitals through the emergency department.[40] In this trial, each patient's EMR[41] ran with a companion piece of software taught to recognize the known signs of septic shock—low blood pressure, elevated heart rate, fever, and a high white blood cell count—and alert the provider.

Let's say that morning blood work on an unconscious patient showed a high white cell count. Lab workers entered that information into the patient's EMR as soon as the tests were completed. Then a nurse doing her rounds 30 minutes later pulls up the patient's EMR again to enter the vital signs she has just taken. The patient is still unconscious and not complaining, but the low blood pressure and slightly elevated heart rate that the nurse enters to the EMR cause a bright yellow pop-up screen to cover the patient's record: a septic shock warning. With a click on that screen, the provider goes to a "best-practices advisory" for sepsis that will lead her step by step through further diagnostic and treatment practices.

---

40. We limit the scope of every experiment so that we can find the kinks and plan effectively for rollout to the larger organization, should the countermeasure prove successful.

41. Electronic medical records. At ThedaCare, we use the EPIC system and run all requests and analysis through our decision resources department.

In this way, we hope to diagnose more sepsis cases earlier while ensuring that best-practice treatment plans are readily available for providers.

The team's target was to reduce sepsis mortality cases by 20% in the first year. After four months of this work, sepsis mortality was down by 21.7% and on a steady decline. With cautious optimism, the team began moving the new ideas and standard work, called BPA for best-practices advisories, to our other major hospital's E.D. patients to see whether the results were reproducible.

In the beginning, teams may need to measure *process metrics* when working through large projects. In the above example, for instance, the team began by measuring how many times the sepsis advisory screen was tripped and then what percentage of the time users clicked through to the best-practices advisory. This is all valuable information, particularly at the unit level, as teams experiment with creating sustainable processes. However, *outcomes* are the real objective.

Ultimately, we always want scorecards to reflect whether we are driving down the defects—in this case, incidence of sepsis. Remember the difference between goals and targets? Eliminating septic shock is the goal; driving down incidence of missed sepsis symptoms is the immediate target.

A general rule of thumb might be that unit-level scorecards often contain targets but all are driving toward the goals of True North. If an obstetrics unit wants to improve the decision-to-incision time on Caesarian section from 33 minutes to 20, that is their target toward the stated goal of improving the quality of patient outcomes.

The highest-level scorecards at ThedaCare are created after the board of trustees' annual strategy sessions. Once the board has confirmed the goals of the True North, the leaders of each division—hospitals, primary care, and hospice—decide the top five or 10 measures their division will focus on in alignment with True North goals. Next, the division vice presidents get together with their managers to write unit-level scorecards that are also focused on True North goals. Then, in conjunction with staff on the front line and their advisory teams, managers begin thinking about and selecting the systemic improvement projects that will move the needle on those division measures and, ultimately, ThedaCare's True North. (Part of a division-level scorecard is included in the appendix, figure 11.)

Think of it as a group of people discussing a common goal, conferring about what each person will do to further the groups' progress. The owner of a car might announce the destination, while one passenger offers to fill up the tank with gas while someone else plots the route and makes snacks. All of it is necessary to get anywhere. It may look as though every unit has its own concerns or separate tasks, but these all feed into the organization's goals.

We have created three easy rules for managers to remember in creating unit-level scorecards.

1. Every target must be measurable by data. Targets are never written as "Create better quality for patients." Instead, this would be "Reduce decision-to-incision time by 30%."

2. We must see performance data quickly. This means we must see measurable changes on a weekly or monthly basis, not annually. If a unit-level team were working toward better HAT[42] scores, for instance, we would not use team members' body mass index scores as a metric because these numbers generally change slowly over time. Also, measuring BMI on a weekly basis could be damaging to morale.

---

42. Health assessment test, or HAT, scores are used to gauge the relative health of employees and are often used to control healthcare insurance costs.

Instead, we would find ways to measure steps per day or participation in a fun exercise program.

3. We must have targets that will drive the True North Metrics. The current rule in our hospitals is that five out of six drivers on every scorecard must relate to a True North category. The sixth might be specific to the unit and would not need to move the needle on True North goals. In this way, we try to keep everyone focused on common True North goals while offering flexibility for unit-level needs.

When thinking about creating scorecards, it is also important to remember how information flows. Intelligence comes from the front line, and this is where we should get most of our facts. We also lean toward the lower-tech solutions for fact gathering—or data collection—such as observation and counting by hand when possible.

Improvement teams will need some computerized data from finance and human resources groups, for instance, but I would strongly urge any hospital not to get distracted by shiny new software that will claim to do analysis for you. In the beginning, it is almost always better to pull that frontline data or facts by hand. Save the big, fancy data-mining programs until your organization is ready—until you are becoming an organization of problem solvers. ThedaCare was nine years into its lean transformation before we got the fancy data analytics program, and I am glad we waited. By staying away from complicated software, we were constantly reminded that these are human efforts. We talk about pushing the needle and drivers for our units, but what we are always talking about at a fundamental level is people, discovering and addressing problems.

Once scorecards are created and displayed on every unit and executive office, you will have accomplished one of the primary objectives of scorecards: making the work visible and therefore draining some of the emotion out of the constant push for improvement. When scorecards are displayed as common targets, I have noticed, the issues around creating change become less personal. A unit, a manager, or I might *own* the scorecard or specific drivers. And that scorecard might show wobbly progress or countermeasures that are not working. But the work on display belongs to all of us. Nobody is personally judged because we are all invested in the outcome.

Let's return to our former truck guy and data miner extraordinaire, Shawn Chartier, for a good illustration of this. Now our director of decision resources, Shawn had a number of roles with us in the beginning and at one time was the manager of ThedaCare's spine business. His responsibilities included the entire flow of patients moving through spine treatments. Shawn was also managing the business of spine care, of course, and one of the drivers on his scorecard was a targeted 10% increase in spine pain treatment, year over year. If previous ratios remained constant, the treatment target would translate into a 5% increase in spine surgery.

That first year, as Shawn prepared to create A3s on his drivers, he pulled the numbers and saw that spine surgeries were down 20% for the year to date—a big backward step away from his target. So, Shawn and his team set about investigating. They compared surgeries by physician and found they were all about the same. They looked at surgeries by type and saw that lumbar fusions were flat compared to the prior year and that cervical fusions were flat but discectomies had dropped steeply. Compared to the previous year, there was a 60% decrease in the surgery to remove herniated disc material that is pressing on nerve roots or the spinal cord.

The team dug further and discovered that all providers and payers were showing the same decrease, so the cause was not a physician group taking their surgeries elsewhere or an insurance group refusing to pay for this procedure. Shawn finally took his investigation to the Wisconsin Hospital Association's massive database of all surgeries in the state and found the same result: a big drop in volume on discectomies everywhere. After consulting with surgeons, the team concluded that the reduction in discectomies was most likely linked to the increase in spinal injections to relieve pain, which Shawn had also uncovered in the WHA database.

Armed with this new information, Shawn and his supervising vice president lowered his targeted volume for surgeries, knowing that it was the only logical course of action. The overall target of 10% growth in spine treatments remained the same.

I shudder to think about what might have happened in the past. Even a valued employee could have been judged incompetent for failing to meet a stated goal and losing ground in treatment volume that first year. And Shawn would have suffered that judgment alone. In the past—as a traditional hospital—we set targets for employees that were written only on performance reviews and then were locked away as a personnel matter. Without those real data the team collected and without the insights of the surgeons, we might have quietly downgraded Shawn's future with ThedaCare. Instead, we saw Shawn's talent with data mining and his ability to teach others the same and promoted him to director of decision resources.

This is one of the most counterintuitive aspects of the business performance system: creating and publicly displaying improvement targets for a unit or division actually protect a leader from unfair judgment. The scorecard limits the number of initiatives and prioritizes among those chosen, helping us to focus our work and to finally see—to collectively see—how we are doing.

Another counterintuitive result of this work? We have discovered that standard work sets us free. But that is for the next chapter.

# Chapter 11

# Standard
## Work for Leaders

"For me, standard work is my road map. It is what drives me through every day," Vicki Van Epps says. "If I didn't have standard work, honestly, I don't know what I would do."

That statement will worry some people, I know. Let me assure you that Vicki can think for herself and does not need a highly structured environment in order to function. Supervisor of our radiation oncology clinic and a 23-year veteran of clinical and leadership work, Vicki has simply found that the framework of standard work has set her free.

To understand this seeming dichotomy, let's follow Vicki through her day. There are a couple of facts to remember as we take this tour. "Standard work" can refer to the current best-known way to complete a task and to the structure or schedule of a leader's day. It might help newcomers to think of the former as "process standard work" and the latter as "schedule standard work," but we just use the one term for both. In each case, standard work is written down and regularly audited. Process standard work can be changed only by team agreement. Also, remember that the supervisor's role and responsibilities in the radiation oncology clinic are largely unchanged since we moved to the business performance system. The supervisor is still expected to know everything that is happening in the clinic or unit, help address any problems that arise, and make sure that staffing meets demand and that patients are well cared for. What has changed is the method used. To put a point on it: now there *is* a method.

"From 8:00 until 9:00 every morning, my day starts at gemba," Vicki says. "I circulate through the clinic,[43] saying good morning to the nurses and therapists and physicists, looking at schedules, and asking general questions."

When Vicki arrives at the reception area, she settles in for a more substantive chat with the administrative associates, whom she calls the eyes and ears of the clinics. From a tick list memorized through daily usage, she asks what the associates are hearing from patients coming in. Is the sidewalk icy? Maybe somebody on staff has a little cough and needs to be reminded to wear a mask. And what does staffing look like for the day? Vicki asks what associates are hearing from doctors. Has someone asked for her patients to be shuffled and her afternoon blocked out? Anything else on the calendar? Students coming in for clinical observations? Vendors making a call? Patients coming in after hours?

Armed with notes from her walkthrough and visit to the associates, Vicki is then ready to run her 9 a.m. stat sheet conference. Hers is a little unusual in that the conversation has as many as six people, including two lead radiation therapists, the lead nurse, the lead physicist, and her manager. Also, Vicki runs the conference instead of her manager most of the time. This clinic has had years of experience with the business performance system and made some changes to fit the work flow.

---

43. Open from 7 a.m. to 5 p.m., this clinic has 25 people on staff, not including Vicki and her manager.

The basic script is the same as any other stat sheet, however, as Vicki leads the discussion through safety, quality, customer service, people, cost, and the wrap-up. Vicki asks which patients might need additional hydration, how they can cover staffing after hours, and where she may need to coordinate with other departments. This conference lasts 15 minutes.

By 9:20 a.m., Vicki can be relatively assured of being back in her office, following up on staff needs, coordinating with her peers, proactively planning her day. This is the time when she usually checks on the progress of her major improvement projects and updates her area improvement center and huddle boards. She may also pull standard work from the kamishibai board and observe the work in action. Since this time is still within our mandated 8–10 a.m. no-meeting zone, Vicki knows that she can focus on the needs of her clinic without getting pulled away.

At 11:30 a.m., it is time for the huddle, which all members of the clinic, including physicians, are encouraged to attend if patient care permits. It is also a 15-minute meeting, performed standing up in front of the huddle board. Like every other huddle in the hospitals, this team discusses new improvement ideas, current projects, and the team's progress toward their goals. Vicki keeps a timer going on her huddle, and when that bell dings, the meeting is over and whatever conversation was happening is shelved for the following day or continued in another setting.

Finished with the huddle by 11:45 a.m., Vicki has just enough time to collect her thoughts and get to one of the noon staff meetings that also define her week. On Tuesdays it is the Tumor Board meeting, for instance, and on Wednesdays she goes to a patient-chart review meeting with physicians.[44]

---

44. Vicki's schedule looks a lot like a manager's schedule in that she runs stat sheet meetings and huddles while her manager, Karen Flom, provides support. This is often what happens after a team is experienced with the business performance system and people take on various roles based on needs and availability.

At 3 p.m., she is back at gemba asking her staff how the day went. Did they have the support they needed? Was anything missing or awry? She captures their comments for future improvement projects, reasons to celebrate the team's work, and any immediate adjustments that need to be made. Because she does this afternoon gemba walk every day, Vicki says, this feels more like chatting than a formal interview. Staff members know that she will be there asking about their days and that she will help them turn frustrations into improvement opportunities.

"Some people might think this sounds repetitive, day after day, but for me this structure means there is no guessing," Vicki says. "I know where I might have capacity in my week to get extra things done. And if I do not have capacity—because the really important aspects of my job are set in my calendar—I do not feel as bad about saying no."

Standard work in Vicki's schedule leaves her secure in knowing that she is doing what she needs to do, when she needs to do it. The fact that standard work also guides each of her tasks means there is no second-guessing.

Vicki's manager, Karen Flom, agrees. For her, standard work means that she has all her most important work hardwired into her day and week: teaching and mentoring team members such as Vicki, addressing problems both immediate and long term with her team, pushing improvements forward, following through on problems, and anticipating needs.

Karen's standard work looks much like Vicki's. The major difference is that, as manager of cancer services and another 25 people outside of the radiation oncology clinic, she has more than one huddle and stat sheet conference happening every morning. She splits time among her groups based on need and on a standardized rotation schedule.

Karen begins each morning at gemba, walking through one or more areas that she manages, collecting information that will help her anticipate the issues of the day. She has a stat sheet meeting and at least one huddle—both of which she is either leading or observing—and then is expected to work through her own list of coaching, observation, and teaching lean tools, as well as interface with doctors and colleagues from other departments. At least once a week, Karen also has a stat sheet meeting with her boss, a VP.

The daily standard work for all managers lists items such as "Plan an intentional conversation with an individual staff member that shows you support staff and their work." Also, "Every day audit a piece of standard work, and twice a week do this with your supervisor." Individual managers then schedule those line items into their work, to suit the flow of their clinics or units, but every manager's morning contains the same three items: gemba, stat sheet meeting, huddle. In each case, the manager is either leading the work or observing and mentoring a supervisor or clinical lead as they lead.

For Karen, the revelation of standard work has been the way that it has helped spread the weight of problem solving. Her desk used to be a repository for problems. People threw things at her—metaphorically—and walked away. Meanwhile, she always felt bad about the things that slipped through her fingers.

"In the old world, in the way we used to manage, there were a ton of things on your desk and not everything got follow-through," Karen says. "Now, we have a system of follow-up that is not wholly dependent on me and my to-do list. It has taken away the onus that I was supposed to be the person remembering everything."

Karen's boss, meanwhile, is also spending part of each morning at gemba—just like all vice presidents. Rotating throughout their areas of responsibility, vice presidents are a common sight now in every clinic and unit. Instead of cause for alarm, staff know the VP is there to observe, find barriers to knock down, and prepare for his or her own stat sheet conference with a manager.

Because every VP is responsible for a handful of small businesses instead of just the one, their focus is always on coaching the business owner, i.e., the manager, on ways to be more effective, teaching him or her to see new issues, and looking for ways to move the improvement needle. So, every morning the VP sits down with one of his or her managers to talk through the same categories—safety, quality, delivery (or customer service), people, and cost—and a wrap-up that includes questions such as, "What trends are you seeing in the stat sheet data?"

Every week the VP also audits his or her clinics or units for their adherence to business performance system practices. Using a simple yes/no survey, the VP asks whether the unit's team is achieving goals, if the unit is improving, if the team is stable. We ask whether the unit is making performance and problems visual, if the huddle board is up-to-date, whether there is evidence of active PDSA problem solving and other signs of a healthy system. This way, we cement the behaviors of our system into routine.

The chief operating officer has standard work that focuses on developing the vice presidents. The COO meets weekly with each VP, stat sheet in hand, to talk about the work and needs of the VPs' units. The COO also meets each week with all VPs to hear executive summaries of their improvement work and observes a number of huddles and VP/manager stat sheet meetings to help guide the VPs' leadership development.

As for my standard work, I begin each Monday morning with the team of VPs to discuss the week ahead and any improvement work that may need extra attention. My goal is to make very formal, standardized visits to gemba four times a month, on top of my more frequent, informal visits.

As president, I know that my presence on a unit or in a clinic is closely watched. No matter how frequently they see me, people are still aware of my position. So I try to use that attention to my advantage, always noting and discussing the few critical measures I want to highlight: safety, cleanliness, and improvement work that is worthy of celebration. When I see something that needs work at gemba, however, I try to make sure that I discuss it later with the area's VP. I discuss safety and cleanliness, but my purpose is not to do any individual coaching or make anyone feel like the president has chewed him out. Negative attention is easier to take from a one-up than from the president.

It is important to remember that standard work is not just a calendar or a script of questions and answers. It is not just the detailed instructions for setting up a huddle board or a leadership advisory team, although standard work includes those things, too. This work is really about how we are standardizing our responses to problems. Whether it is a sudden emergency or a shift in a unit's focus that is at issue, standard work helps make our reactions knowable and less frantic.

Let me illustrate with two related stories of before and after. When I became a vice president in 2005, I was determined to be hands-on and close to the work. We were already rolling out lean tools, and I knew that my place was at gemba. That first week on the job, I went up to the inpatient oncology unit just to have a look around and see whether there were any barriers that needed my attention.

The look on the faces of nurses and therapists as I passed them on the floor was unmistakable. I could almost hear them whispering in my wake, "What's she doing here? It must be really bad." My presence meant bad news. It was a horrible, isolating feeling.

Not long after that, I received an automatically generated incident report about a fall in that same unit that resulted in a death 30 days earlier. I was astounded that this was the first I was hearing about it. I went back to the unit asking, "What are we going to do about this?" I was not even sure whether this was a case of a patient dying and then falling or falling and, because of that, dying. It is a critical distinction.

Leaders in the unit told me not to worry. They had a team scheduled to consider root-cause analysis of the incident in two weeks. I accepted the team's course of action—this was early in the days of our lean transformation, and we were not always nimble—but I knew there had to be a better way.

Seven years later, 2012, I received a call that there had been an incident in one of our operating rooms. An unconscious, anesthetized patient had been "assisted to the floor" from a surgical table less than an hour earlier. This is a nice way of saying a patient fell off the operating table but had been caught by a nurse before hitting the ground. The nurse had immediately notified her clinical lead of the incident, and the lead set in motion the standardized containment plan: the patient was moved to another table in another operating room while the incident site was shut down.

The surgical manager called me to say they needed to do a root-cause analysis right away, before they could open that operating room again, and asked if I could get a lean facilitator to assist. Later, the team would also ask for the funds to get a new fracture-style operating table to replace the one that malfunctioned. My role was to do the work appropriate to my position: supplying the team with the personnel and funds needed to correct the situation.

One kind of incident response became another, better kind of response because of standard work. In the second case, all knew their roles and nobody had fear in reporting the incident because they knew that their colleagues would look for root causes and not scapegoats.

Standardized responses mean that our process was less judgmental and we could get to root cause without people fearing that blame would fall on them because they were in the vicinity.

We should be clear, however, that we are not completely free of problems created by people. When we search for root cause in an open and honest manner, we find that the process is to blame 95% of the time. That means 5% of the time, a person is at fault, and we should not sugarcoat that fact. When standard work exists and the person is at fault, we find that one of three conditions usually exists: the person has not been trained in the standard work, the standard work is wrong, or the person decided not to follow it.

If we have an objective process and it uncovers a person willfully ignoring standard work, then we must be open about coaching that person. Occasionally, people will underperform or create errors that require them to leave the organization. We do not celebrate that fact, but we follow through for the sake of everyone else who performs diligently. And because our investigations into errors were open and standardized—investigations are nothing more than A3s—there were few mysteries.

Standard work has been a big help in other personnel issues, as well. Like most healthcare organizations, we were always promoting great nurses and therapists out of clinical work and then coaching them to become leaders. Before standardization, the quality of coaching was entirely reliant on the availability and ability of the coach. As MaryJeanne Schaffmeyer points out, following standard work can guide new leaders to places they never imagined. In this case, it was the night shift.

"This is a good example of how standard work helps us, because we all know how hard it can be for newly promoted people to differentiate in their new role, to lead people who were, last week, their coworkers,"

MaryJeanne says. "And this one nurse in obstetrics, she really wanted to challenge herself and become a supervisor. She had a lot of leadership skills, but she was being promoted at around the same time that we needed to change the schedule and have everyone take a turn on night shifts."

At the time, we allowed seniority to dictate the nursing schedule. The most experienced nurses, therefore, were almost all working daytime hours during the week while newer hires dominated the schedule in the middle of the night and on weekends. Doctors had begun to complain about a lack of experienced nurses for middle-of-the-night deliveries, and they had a point. If babies do not respect the clock, age and experience, we should not either. Still, telling our most experienced nurses to go back to the overnight shifts was going to be controversial.

"This new supervisor came to me and said, 'You don't understand how the staff is going to feel about this!' She was really upset. I just looked at her and said, 'I don't want you to care about that.' And I will never forget the look on her face when I said that. She looked like she had been slapped," MaryJeanne says.

"The thing is being a leader means sometimes taking your people where they do not want to go. So I could not let her care about feelings right then. Instead, we sat down and worked on incorporating questions into her stat sheet that would help her get the answers from her team."

MaryJeanne pulled out one tool after another—stat sheets, huddles, A3s, visual management, and advisory teams—to help this new supervisor see how to work through the problem, one step at a time, with her team. At stat sheet conferences, she was asking her manager, "How are we going to staff the night shift if nobody wants to work it?" At huddle, she was asking, "How can we find a good mix of experience on the night shift so it is not all new people?" And before too long, the more experienced nurses that the new supervisor was now leading were helping her find the answers and the confidence to lead her team to exactly where they needed to go: the night shift.

"I think that's when I understood, really, the power of what we were doing," MaryJeanne says. "When I saw this young woman become more of a leader and less of a protector, I knew."

Standard work has also changed longtime leaders such as MaryJeanne and me. In the old world, we prided ourselves on being problem solvers. You had a question? We had answers. And it felt wonderful to be the person walking through the room with all the answers—shooting from the hip, knowing the quick fix for any situation. In private moments, we would admit to doubt. But on the floor, we were invincible.

Our jobs now are quite different. In a business performance system, the leader is more of a Zen master. Even if we "know" the answer, our conclusion is less valuable than a team's investigation into root cause, learning the tools, applying the logic, and applying their own solution.

Instead of rapping out answers, we have now become listeners. We may suggest tools to apply and offer inputs, but we do not have *the answer*. Answers are the province of teams, applying tools in a standardized process. It works much better than our off-the-cuff retorts—no matter how learned or experienced.

Of course, it was not easy giving up those roles. We have talked about the work we had to do on ourselves, to stop blurting "the answer" and become mentors instead.[45] Perfection is always outside our grasp, it

---

45. I do not mean to imply that command and control is never appropriate. In an emergency—a power outage, a huge influx of emergency victims—that style of leadership can be essential to managing the situation. In daily situations in which we are attempting to develop our teams and leaders, however, it is mentoring that's needed.

seems, but all of us who have been through this process have become more patient, more compassionate. The work demands it of us.

Standard work actually demands quite a bit, and some of it is contradictory. For instance, I know that I must be rigidly fixed to my standard work calendar and processes in order to be flexible in my thinking about problems. When I have a problem now, I do not get stuck on the fact of my problem. (A patient fell off a table!) I help others move immediately into developing a hypothesis and testing it. We found we could knock down issues much faster because we all agreed on a standard way to problem solve.

Now that everyone knows our role on gemba, leaders do not get the worried looks we used to get. I doubt anyone asks, "What's she doing here?" They know that it is my job to be there, observing, knocking down barriers, helping in the work. I am still the boss, but people seem much more comfortable talking to me now. We have all found freedom in these defined roles.

What I have described here is the *what* of standard work. Some readers will still be wondering *why*, however. Why go through the upheaval and energy of creating and sustaining standardized processes for leaders? One enormous benefit we have not discussed is organizational communication.

When our hospitals work well, I think of the entire division as an atmospheric system. Data generated at the front line—the facts on the ground—rise through the organization like water evaporating from a lake. Strategies and decisions, meanwhile, rain down from above. A business performance system is the cloud where information gathers and mixes with strategy to inform everyone's decisions. Continuous improvement is an organizing principle for that cloud, ensuring that good information is rising and that company strategy is guiding our work.

Just as continuous improvement is an organizing principle, so is standard work. In many ways, standard work is the glue that holds our business performance system together, day in and day out. We know what is expected of us; we know what to expect of others.

The physicians at ThedaCare have noticed the difference in every clinic and unit as the business performance system has been adopted. Let's look next at how this system changes work flow for doctors and other providers and their role in the world driven by collaboration and standard work.

# Chapter 12

# Bringing
## Physicians into the Fold

Think about going to see your family doctor to talk about a strange new pain or rash. You wait, sitting on the exam table in a flimsy paper gown until your doctor enters the room, washes her hands at the sink and asks over her shoulder, "What seems to be the trouble?" Thus begins the most common A3 problem-solving cycle in healthcare, says Dr. James McGovern, medical director of Theda Clark Medical Center.

"We always start with the current-state, understanding a person's symptoms and conditions, taking into account his or her medical history from the electronic medical record (EMR). Then we develop a differential diagnosis, which is like the problem statement," says Dr. McGovern. "If we don't know what's wrong with the patient, we do a gap analysis, asking many questions and ordering tests to determine what else we need to know in order to make the diagnosis." (Plan)

After this investigation into the current state of our patient's health, a physician creates a plan of care that may include medications, physical therapy, or surgery. (Do) The next morning during rounds or next week in the office, the doctor revisits the patient and evaluates the treatment's effectiveness. (Study) Based on that evaluation, the doctor adjusts or continues the present management. (Act/Adjust) The next visit, the cycle starts over again.

"Essentially, we are doing an A3 with every patient we see," Dr. McGovern tells his fellow doctors. "Maybe our physicians don't know the terms PDSA or A3, but we are all using the same scientific method."

There are many similarities between lean and the work of physicians. We all use the scientific method; we depend on experimentation to advance the work. Patient care comes first. And, yet, there are many disconnects between doctors and continuous improvement, too. Since beginning our transformation to lean and rolling out the business performance system, we have found many roadblocks to fully integrating our physicians in the work and a few simple methods for overcoming the dissonance.

First, we must note the obvious importance of compensation. Physicians employed by ThedaCare have a greater interest in adapting to these new methods of working. We can tie bonuses to performance improvements and write job descriptions to include a certain amount of capacity to perform improvement work. Healthcare systems with employed physicians may therefore have an easier time integrating everyone into the system. But at ThedaCare, as at many health systems, the majority (70%) of doctors who work in our hospitals are independent, and they like it that way. There are fewer opportunities to pull these doctors into lean improvement work. So we must learn to lead by influence and demonstrate results that benefit the physicians as well as ThedaCare. Fortunately, administrators and providers share a central goal: improving patient outcomes and experience.

Also there is an issue of working styles. Physicians typically are skeptical, resistant to change, and comfortable only with approaches learned during the course of their professional training. From the time they are in medical school, physicians are trained to rely on particular mental algorithms in order to make the assured, accurate decisions on which we rely. And those algorithms can vary significantly, depending on where the doctor trained. One physician might value speed-to-treatment, while a close associate strongly distrusts the first solution because skepticism and further inquiry were part of his training.

Team discussions, therefore, often need to back up and begin with talking out our basic assumptions—another frustration for time-starved physicians even if they are sympathetic to the idea of continuous improvement. I understand how vexing it can be to adopt team deci-sion making, to work in situations where it might take hours to agree on the problem and the countermeasures, and then weeks or months to see the results of those efforts. But this is the working style of a lean organization: methodical, inclusive, deliberate.

Many of us in healthcare administration suffer from a malady similar to that of our physicians. Administrators and physicians alike learn to be quick with a definitive answer when asked a question. Dr. McGovern calls it "jumping to solutions." On my team, we call it "a solution look-ing for a problem," and we often jokingly refer to this when we see it happening. But then someone will ask, "Do you know the root cause?" or "What is your hypothesis?" Physicians new to this style of problem solving may take some time to adjust. And as Jill Menzel, business unit manager of the hospitalist program, notes, there may be plenty of eye rolling along the way.

A chemical engineer by training, Jill came to us from the paper industry, where she was working to implement a combination of lean and Six Sigma. Then in 2008, she heard former ThedaCare CEO John Toussaint, MD give a talk about our lean transformation, and she jumped ship into healthcare. She immediately recognized the looks that physicians gave her as the same ones she got from operators in the paper mill—the looks that say, *Oh, here we go again with the Japanese words and the continuous improvement.* It turns out that people with expertise and long experience can be pretty inflexible, no matter what their field.

Jill started out at ThedaCare as a lean facilitator, working in various parts of the organization before becoming a leader in operations. She saw that doctors liked the results of lean, even if they did not like the terminology or the time required. Physicians liked better patient care and better outcomes. They liked it when kaizen teams—which included physicians—helped to eliminate medication reconciliation errors or cut in half the amount of time it took to get cardiac patients the angioplasty needed to save their lives. Good results, Jill saw, were levers to acceptance and involvement.

Jill can now offer a simple and important piece of advice on introducing physicians to a business performance system and integrating them into the work: lead with results.

"I know they laugh at me," Jill says. "And they really do not want to hear the theories behind the work. That's fine. They want results. So we make sure that any problems physicians have get brought up in the huddle. We address their issues as a team and find countermeasures."

Jill has found that hospitalist huddles for physicians look a little different from the unit-based huddles. The New Improvement Opportunity slips that you would find on physician huddle boards will target different problems from a unit board because they relate to the clinician experience. Working with Dr. McGovern, Jill convenes a hospitalist huddle once a week. This team usually includes two or three physicians, two physician assistants or nurse practitioners, and a few members of administrative staff.

Examples of things they have tackled include work flow clashes between physicians, implementing new clinical protocols for conditions such as sepsis or pneumonia, standard work around Bedside Care Conferences,[46] and a lot of staffing-to-demand issues. Jill's team and the physicians determine targets and time lines together in a process we call How Much by When. This makes explicit to the whole team who will be working through the A3, and when the issues will be reviewed in a future huddle. We find that this kind of clarity has helped encourage physicians to attend the huddles, get involved, and help improve performance.

"We just kept working our tools, improving processes, and over time our physicians learned to appreciate it," Jill says. "We're creating pull for the results we can deliver, and creating pull for lean and the business performance system more generally."

With more physicians attending huddles, knowledge of the system spreads, and physicians find ways to work within the system. As Dr. McGovern says, physicians are learning that in order to have a voice in how improvements—or any changes—happen in the hospitals, they need to work within the business performance system.

Still, Jill and Dr. McGovern manage the hospitalists, who are employed by ThedaCare. The other 70% of accredited physicians working in our hospitals are a different challenge. Mark Hermans, MD, vice president of medical affairs, essentially oversees those doctors and works with two deputies: Dr. McGovern, who is medical director for Theda Clark Medical Center and the hospitalists, and Clark "Buzz" Boren, MD, medical director of Appleton Medical Center and all surgical services.

---

46. Bedside Care Conferences are what we call rounding at ThedaCare and include a physician, nurse/case manager, pharmacist, and social workers or other caregivers, if needed. Family members are invited, as well, so that there is agreement and a common understanding of the plan of care.

The three doctors went through business performance system training together and agree that one tool, more than others, has been useful for driving improvement and winning over physicians. While stat sheets have been problematic for doctors and their hectic morning schedules, the huddle boards show—publicly, transparently—what issues are being addressed and how. Physicians are learning that huddles are where issues go to be resolved.

"I can't say that physicians are coming to our huddles in droves. But that is mostly due to time constraints," Dr. Hermans says. Respect for their time is essential. "So we let them know when an issue they raised is being discussed at the medical affairs huddle, and we talk about results." If a physician cannot attend the huddle, a team member is assigned to follow up with the doctor and report on any progress or decisions.

In years past, Dr. Hermans was the problem-solving resource for the complaints of medical staff, which include the hundreds of independent physicians who work in our hospitals. Back then, I worried about the stress of that job. I imagined it would be very difficult to be perceived as *the* person to conduct investigations and find solutions for every problem related to our physicians. I wondered how long until he burned out. I asked, "Who would really want that job?" We had to find a better way.

With the business performance system, physician issues are now routinely routed through Dr. Hermans's twice-weekly medical affairs team huddles using the standard New Improvement Opportunity slip. These physician-generated slips are combined with other improvement ideas at the huddle board, and, as you can imagine, the number of New Improvement Opportunity slips grows each week as physicians become more accustomed to the system. And with more slips coming in, there is need for prioritization.

"We use the PICK chart to help us decide between quick projects and what will take time. We usually figure that anything that might take a couple of hours and can be done within seven days is a *just do it*. More than that, we start an A3," Dr. Hermans says.[47]

With every complaint he receives from a physician, Dr. Hermans explains how the complaint will be addressed, how the huddle works, and what the probable time line is. When the complaint or new improvement opportunity is due to be discussed in the huddle, the physician is invited to attend. So, with every problem, there is an opportunity to introduce doctors to the business performance system and talk about using the scientific method for problem solving.

This does not mean, of course, that the huddle board in medical affairs is populated only by complaints or sour grapes. Dr. Hermans has drivers for safety, quality, people, and financial improvements, just like everyone else. And the huddles are useful for dealing with all kinds of emerging issues.

Not long after Dr. Hermans began his Tuesday and Thursday huddles, for instance, a trauma patient arrived at one of our rural hospitals, was given an incomplete initial exam, and was then sent to the wrong main hospital. The patient received good care and was fine, but the physicians noticed the gap in protocol and saw a potential disaster.

Dr. Hermans addressed the situation in huddle. It was definitely not a quick-fix project. The team began an A3 and launched countermeasures, including new training and standard work for the rural hospital and new standard work for the movement of trauma patients, ensuring

---

47. Another standard we commonly use to decide whether to start an A3 is the rule of threes. If the improvement can be accomplished with three people or fewer in three steps or fewer over three days or fewer, it is a quick fix or a "just do it." More than three in any category and we open a new A3.

that every patient goes to the hospital with the best resources for his or her problems.

"I know the physicians were happy we were going out and dealing with the issue," Dr. Hermans says.

Two or three days a week, Dr. Hermans also goes to gemba. He and his team will pick a unit to visit, based on perceived need or random choice. The team usually meets with the manager and reads both the huddle board and the area improvement center. After review, they talk to providers in the area, looking for any issues that medical affairs can address in the huddle.

When physicians see this kind of focused approach to problems, their initial complaints about lean tools start to fall away. Doctors who used to grumble about standard work as a slippery slope to "cookbook medicine" start to see that standardized, coordinated responses to emergency situations such as cardiac arrests and strokes mean that patients get treatment faster, Dr. Hermans says. Attitudes are changing.

ThedaCare had been on a lean journey for six years before we began this work, and I have seen that physicians usually progress from active resistance to grumbling and then finally to adoption of the new language. We might have been able to move further and faster if we had modified the language from the beginning, as new jargon can be off-putting. Providers can be particularly defensive about the language attached to lean thinking. They hear words associated with the Toyota Production System and say, *That's not for us. We don't make widgets.*

My advice to organizations beginning a lean journey would be to recast a lot of the Japanese words into language that medical providers already use. Instead of kamishibai, we could have simply said "observation schedules." If we wanted to be cute, we could have called the board the "observation deck." Whatever words we chose, finding familiar terms to reflect the work would likely have made for easier acceptance.

By now, there are some readers wondering why anyone should go to the trouble to incorporate doctors into a business performance system. Physicians grumble about new words; they want quick solutions, while lean work is methodical and very process oriented. Why not simply do our improvement work around the physicians?

As president of the hospitals, one of my privileges is being able to observe huddles throughout the organization. From radiology to obstetrics to housekeeping, watching a team brainstorm about improving work environments is inspiring. A physician huddle can be something else again. Doctors may not like using lean terms or following a formal procedure, but when a few brilliant minds are focused on the same clinical issue, that huddle becomes rich with detail and logical leaps that move the work far and fast. If the word "awesome" was not so overused, that is how I would describe some physician huddles I have seen.

There is another even more compelling reason to integrate physicians into a business performance system, though: they need it, and so do we. We are in this together. The healthcare industry can no longer count on being paid in the old fee-for-service model. The country simply cannot afford it. The new value-based model called for in the Affordable Care Act—and already being adopted in pieces by the country's largest payer, Medicare—focuses on paying physicians and hospitals for good outcomes instead of individual procedures. As Dr. Buzz Boren puts it, we are moving from the volume world to a value world, and it will be a bumpy trip.

"Right now, physicians may not think that BPS is a very good fit," says Dr. Boren, who practiced surgery for nearly 40 years before becoming a medical director. "We're living in a world where time is money, where success is predicated on doing more procedures, more tests. Physicians don't take the time nor are they paid to learn the lean BPS tools and apply them to their offices and practices. Until we change the way physicians are reimbursed, we will struggle at this."

The good news for those struggling to align physicians with lean and a business performance system is that reimbursement changes are coming at us fast. Medicare and the Affordable Care Act are moving the industry rapidly toward a value model, where healthcare providers will make money based on how well they improve quality of care and eliminate waste. One of the most common proposals for reforming healthcare toward a value model—the population-based payment concept—is being run by Medicare in experiments around the country as of this writing. It is bound to change everything.

Think of a middle-aged man coming in to a hospital for a knee replacement in 2012. Each aspect of his care, from diagnosis to surgery, hardware to physical therapy and his hospital stay, was billed separately at a price negotiated with an insurance company. If something went wrong and the patient needed more treatment, we had a new billable incident. Hospitals and doctors got paid anew for every mistake made, and every provider had a separate, secret agreement with the insurer.

In a population-based payment system, insurers or Medicare pays medical groups a predetermined amount to meet the healthcare needs of an entire population. The populations and payments are risk adjusted, but there is no separate billing for that knee replacement. The health system that provides the most efficient and highest-quality care—no surgical errors, best recovery times—will be the most profitable. The surgeon, hospital, physical therapists, and all other caregivers must coordinate care as well as costs and payments. The largest return will go to the health system that improves its processes until it finds the very best knee replacement, with no waste or do-overs and with the speediest recovery time for that middle-aged man who just wants to get back on his feet.

This payment system will require even more involvement from lean-thinking healthcare administrators, who will need to optimize the processes between medical specialists to increase coordination and reduce waste. Physicians will need to be engaged as well. Doctors will learn that influencing this work will have enormous impact on patient outcomes and their pay. So, the question is how to make the best use of physicians in improvement work, within their hectic schedules and need for quick solutions.

We should work on making some projects a little less deliberative, a little faster, to fit the needs of physicians. Maybe we can script in specific pieces of the work that doctors can drop in on, in order to influence outcomes without spending days at it.

The point is a management system needs to be both flexible and firmly entrenched in the PDSA cycle to adjust and improve performance. We must learn from our mistakes and be prepared to change our tools as new realities and needs surface. Change is, after all, the only constant.

Let's turn to the future then, to a quick look at how this system is likely to change and adapt over time.

Chapter **13**

# The Future
## at Our Door

Patients are the center of our world. These are our neighbors and family members; one day the patients will be you and me. And so it is only right that we begin a discussion of the immediate future of healthcare management systems with the future of our patient population, which is changing rapidly.

Just a few decades ago, hospitals were the centers of catastrophe. We saw victims of sudden illness and accidents. We generally offered short courses of treatment that the patient either survived or did not. For lesser maladies people saw a family doctor and, even there, care was usually targeted at a particular complaint with a limited time horizon.

Now, we have entered into long-term relationships with our patients. Longevity is increasing. Diabetes, obesity, asthma, arthritis, and mental disorders such as depression and bipolar disease now call for regular, ongoing treatments that can last a lifetime. Many cancers are becoming chronic conditions, joining HIV/AIDS as a disease we can live with for decades.

This means that much of healthcare will focus on helping patients to help themselves in managing and improving their lives. Out of absolute necessity, we will finally begin to focus—as an industry—on wellness instead of illness. We will pay more attention to the life needs of the patients, to keeping people independent and able to care for themselves well into old age. This will require new tools and more time and patience. We will spend more time counseling people on how, for instance, specific diets and exercise affect their chronic disease, and our information will be based on solid scientific evidence rather than fads. We will talk more about staying out of the exhausting cycle of hospitalization and recovery and less about what new, short-term treatments we can offer.

We will focus on patient wellness because it is the right thing to do and because we will be paid that way. In the near future, healthcare organizations will most likely receive a pool of funds to look after the healthcare needs of a population of patients, as I noted in the previous chapter. A number of experiments have been running around the United States and the value-based, or population-based, payment concept has emerged as the most likely method for controlling costs while improving patient outcomes and experiences.[48]

Using this system, independent healthcare providers will be profitable only if they offer good care with a minimum of defects[49] and waste. If patients in an organization's population pool suffer from runaway obesity,

---

48. Early experiments have pointed to real troubles, though, when value-based payment systems exist alongside fee-for-service systems. Value-based healthcare organizations actually lose money when a certain percentage of insurers continue to pay fees for service. See the JAMA article *How the Pioneer ACO Model Needs to Change: Lessons from Its Best-Performing ACO* available at createvalue.org/beyondheroes.

49. Defects in this case include missed diagnoses; wrong site surgeries; releasing a patient from hospital too soon, causing a relapse; or any extraneous testing or procedure. Currently, consumers and taxpayers pay for these things. In future, it looks like healthcare organizations will be paying the bill instead. Medicare has already begun eliminating reimbursement for medical error in some situations.

asthma attacks that require hospitalization, and births complicated by a lack of prenatal care, that will cost the organization. A lot. That means we will see a major push by the healthcare industry to offer better preventive care. Physicians and administrators will have a vested interest in knowing which tests and procedures are the most effective for patients, as opposed to the most billable.

So how does this relate to the business performance system? Healthcare organizations that practice continuous improvement will have the advantage in this system because they are already accustomed to increasing profit margins by eliminating waste and creating more efficient processes. If medical group A investigates its treatment path for stroke victims and creates better outcomes by reducing the time it takes to administer clot-busting drugs, for instance, it will spend fewer resources on patient recovery time than group B and therefore earn a better profit margin and reputation. (This will also save the family and community from the costs and heartbreak associated with long-term care of a person who can no longer function at full capacity.) Saving money by offering better treatment also means a medical group could afford to attract the best providers and reinvest in its facilities and people.

Two things I like about the value-based payment concept is that it creates the right incentives to improve quality and will require that we produce reliable quality metrics in order to get paid. Since those data will become public—more on that later—it is not a far leap to assume that most organizations will be required to act upon those data and improve quality as well. The business performance system will serve us well in that it supports the production of quality metrics and provides the framework for staying focused on improvement.

Another thing I like: value-based payments mean we will be required to work well in teams, to coordinate our actions and act collectively in order to create value. This is something the huddle boards, improvement teams, and A3 thinking have been training us to do. It turns out that while we were improving our hospitals, we were learning to work as the future will demand.

All of this will require adjustments for people on both ends of the stethoscope. Doctors will work less independently. They will not scribble notes in a chart and move on. They will need to collaborate with other physicians and care providers, sharing notes through the patient's EMR and meeting to brainstorm on more difficult cases. Physicians will depend on team members to gather information and carry out treatment plans, and they will rely on input from others to write those plans.

Patients—eventually, you and me—will spend less time with physicians and more time with other licensed clinical professionals who have the training to help us wherever we require care, including in our homes. Physicians are the most expensive touch labor employed by healthcare, and the truth is we do not need to see them for every checkup. Also, there are not enough doctors to go around. Some less populated areas of the country lack primary care practitioners—the backbone of healthcare—entirely. A diverse team of medical providers can help extend the physician's capacity and geographic range. Technology can provide some solutions to the physician shortage, such as video conferencing, but we will still need teams of highly trained and certified helpers to interact directly with patients.

This may sound like the physician, who is currently the center of the healthcare universe, will be hamstrung or sidelined. But this model will actually leave physicians free to focus on what they were trained to do: diagnosis, treatment plans, surgery, emergency care, and medical procedures. Instead of spending long appointments talking with patients, trying to understand why a plan of care is not working and what medications are really being taken, physicians will be able to rely on a well-trained team of medical providers, such as nurse practitioners, pharmacists, and various therapists, to gather information, present it to the team, and carry out parts of the care plan. Lean thinking helps us identify value streams and provide better care in shorter time frames, as well as helping to ensure that the right clinician is there to provide care at the right time. The lean management system supports the sustainment and improvement of all of these processes.

Patients with chronic conditions that require long-term treatment will spend the most time with providers such as physical therapists, behaviorists, nutritionists, and pharmacists—even lifestyle coaches—who will support the patient and execute the plan of care. That plan, written by the physician and the care team after diagnosis, will be reviewed and updated in regular team meetings that may look a lot like a huddle or an A3 update. Someday, I expect, those A3 updates will use PDSA thinking to directly address individual patient needs. Teams might gather around something very much like a huddle board to ask how best to address Lori's[50] high cholesterol and depression. Using team knowledge to address patient problems, including information gathered from home visits and phone calls, we may even find new ways to think about and find the root cause of chronic conditions.

Meanwhile, patients need to be able to understand their data and be accountable for their decisions. Patients—especially those with chronic conditions—will be welcomed as members of their own medical team. That means patients will be expected to keep up with necessary testing, know their results, and make a good effort to improve. Technological advances, such as smartphone applications that accomplish simple tests and upload the results directly to an EMR, are already on the horizon and will make some of this patient involvement much easier. Opportunities for self-care will emerge that we cannot even guess at today, and they will

---

50. At ThedaCare, when we talk about the needs of the customer, we find it useful to personalize that customer so we often talk about "Lori's" needs.

be necessary as patients move from passive participants to accountable team members.

Right now, a patient who rolls her eyes at the earnest advice of a physician and continues to smoke three packs of cigarettes a day pays the same insurance premium as a vegan yoga enthusiast of the same age. That might need to change. Patients who work with their teams with an attitude of continuous improvement toward their own health will be rewarded with better results. Those who do not want to work with their medical team are more likely to require emergency interventions and will need to pay fees or accept other consequences that reflect their decisions.

There are many aspects of the coming healthcare system that I cannot foresee, of course. How much tough love are patients going to need to turn the corner toward healthier habits, and what will that tough love look like? By taking waste out of healthcare processes, can we find enough resources to patch shortfalls in the system? Or will we need to find new ways to apportion care with limited resources? The only thing certain is that change is coming because we can no longer afford the national healthcare bill that shoots higher every year as medical technology and longevity advance.

Being an optimist, I believe that we will have a more sensible, affordable healthcare system within the foreseeable future. There will also be a lot of disruption along the way. Whether that system is single payer or some combination of government-sponsored, traditional insurance, and population-based payments, I do not know. Since I spend all my days in hospitals, however, I do know that the payment system influences the delivery system. By moving from a volume (of procedures) system and toward one based on value of care—as I am sure we are doing—we will be able to focus on what really matters and patients will benefit.

Because healthcare companies will need to compete based on the value they offer, we will need to decide the meaning of "value" and how to recognize and reward it. The question of quality can be tricky for any service field. For decades, we have been struggling with how to recognize quality in education, for instance, and which levers to pull to produce better results. There are hundreds of variables and thousands of arguments on how to produce better students. In many ways, healthcare is more straightforward. Fewer hospital-acquired infections are good. Zero infections are better. Shorter recovery time following a joint replacement is good. Infant mortality is bad. Medication reconciliation errors—all drug errors—are bad.

Where we run into issues with transparency and quality is in trying to produce outcomes data. Outcomes are about end results. How are patients doing five years after a heart attack that was treated at hospital A versus hospital B? How do Dr. Smith's hip replacements hold up over time compared to those of other surgeons? We need this information. We need longitudinal data over time to answer many important questions, and much of these data have never been collected. We need this information but are still struggling with how to frame the questions. Do we measure quality outcomes five years after a hip replacement as mobility or pain levels? Deciding the definition of value, and then identifying the necessary data to illustrate value, is a very big challenge.

Here is another challenge: once data are identified and collected, they must be presented in a format understandable to the average American 18-year-old student. Once a person is old enough to make medical decisions as an adult, he or she must have accessible, understandable facts to support those decisions. And they must be inclusive: we need to expand our capture of outcomes data to include healthcare services provided by nontraditional outlets such as pharmacies offering allergy shots and flu vaccines, community gyms that offer physical therapy, and any other organization that influences patient health. We need coordination with these outlets because, at this point, we do not know when our patients get flu shots at the local pharmacy, so we do not know how we are doing against our goal of 100% participation in annual flu shots. Problem-solving teams at ThedaCare have already begun opening and standardizing those channels of communication, but we have far to go.

Letting patients and payers judge providers on quality will require real transparency. This is great news for patients. Knowing how well doctors and hospitals perform, based on facts instead of rumors, will benefit everyone. Imagine being able to select a health system for your family based on health outcomes data or finding a specialist to look at your nagging backache based on the results that three or four local doctors have reported—and others have confirmed—over the past five years.

It is great for the patient, but transparency will also create competition that will stress many organizations. Transparency will clearly differentiate excellent healthcare systems from adequate and inadequate ones. Some organizations will not survive. The good news for excellent healthcare systems that focus on process improvements is that they will be prepared to expand into the gaps created by organizations that cannot compete.

By focusing on wellness, the industry will change dramatically in other ways, too. In decades past, insurance companies have been gatekeepers to hold down costs, deciding which patients can have what procedures and medicines. Epic battles and lawsuits have risen from this tension. If we move to population-based payments—to paying providers to keep a population healthy with the finite resources made available—it will be doctors and administrators in that gatekeeper role. Nobody relishes that idea. The only way we can do this and keep the public trust is through transparency. Once again, transparency of quality and cost data is critical.

And the only way we can achieve transparency, better quality, lower cost, and an organization that will stand up to the coming challenges is through better management of our processes, which is the objective of lean. By using lean tools, we have become comfortable looking at our data—the naked facts of the quality we actually produce—and then finding ways to improve those numbers. Every health organization will need to become similarly comfortable with data and create goals for producing and publishing it in real time.

Creating an entire organization that is comfortable looking at its own data—knowing it will be publicly available—and then acting on it is one of the reasons that we created the business performance system. Anyone can figure out how to capture and disseminate process data. Just hire the right computer genius, right? The real trick is producing and using the data in a way that is helpful for managers and clinicians instead of being threatening and distracting. (We know that clinical business intelligence is a serious gap in this industry; we will all be working on this for a long time.)

Our business performance system has been designed to help managers as they confront the data and then allow those data to lead the continuous improvement work. They provide a framework for improvements to both clinical and administrative work, encouraging everyone to use common sense and the scientific method instead of micromanaging to get work done. All of this is exactly as simple and as complicated as developing, writing, and improving on standard work. Over and over again.

Our business performance system will not solve world hunger. In 10 years, it will not even look exactly as it does today at ThedaCare. As we move forward with continuous improvement, each iteration of our system will help us evolve into the next best practices, with healthcare providers and administrators moving together in the same direction to meet the needs of the patient.

The question for most organizations that understand the pressing needs of the future will be about the first steps of the journey. How do you begin? Instead of telling you, though, how about if I show you?

Toward the end of 2011, the ThedaCare Center for Healthcare Value asked me to develop and teach a course about our business performance system. Then we recruited the COO of the ThedaCare hospitals, MaryJeanne Schaffmeyer, to help teach a one-day overview course for senior healthcare executives who are struggling with managing a lean organization. Later, we added Patsy Engel, Mike Radke, and Jill Menzel to teach a course for middle management. Several organizations went deeper, participating in one or more of the five two-day, in-depth modules we developed on foundational elements of the system. Within the first 12 months, 240 organizations from across North America were represented at these seminars.

So, instead of telling you how to begin converting your management system into one that makes sense for the lean healthcare era, allow me to introduce you to four organizations that have attended ThedaCare Center seminars and then gone home and created their own lean management systems. I have visited each of these organizations to see their progress and know they have important stories to tell.

# Chapter 14

# **Four** Variations on Creating a Lean Management System

As we began achieving significant results with our business performance system in 2010, we also started receiving requests from organizations asking to come and see what ThedaCare was doing. We are a nonprofit health system and we wanted to share everything we could, but we also needed to get our work done. So, we partnered with the nonprofit ThedaCare Center for Healthcare Value[51] to create standardized work for describing what we were doing and why, and to allow gemba visits from leaders of other healthcare organizations. Since 2010, we have had hundreds of such visits, and these interactions have given me a unique opportunity to see how others interpret and then roll out a lean management system. The four organizations depicted in this chapter, who were among the 240 organizations to visit ThedaCare and receive at least some training in the business performance system, offer a range of experiences that will be useful for anyone considering adopting such a system.

---

51. The Center was founded by John Toussaint, MD, former CEO of ThedaCare, author of *On the Mend* and *Potent Medicine*, who was responsible for initiating the lean transformation of ThedaCare.

None of the leaders you will meet in this chapter are heroes. From the CEO of a small hospital in Muscatine, Iowa, to the senior vice president of a major New York City health system, these people and organizations have one important thing in common: a desire to improve and make those improvements stick.

The results are lean management systems that are as unique as the organizations in which they were created. I think it is instructive to point out the systems' similarities as well, but I will save that for after the sketches. First, let's meet leaders from four healthcare organizations and see the very first steps they took toward a lean management system. They offer their lessons learned and generously share what they might do differently next time. Perhaps you will see your own organization reflected here or use a combination of their experiences and ideas to create a unique path that makes sense for your circumstances.

## UnityPoint Health–Trinity Muscatine: Iowa

Like a lot of lean leaders, Jim Hayes began as a dabbler. Back in a very small regional hospital in Greenville, Illinois, where Jim was CEO, he and a few others learned lean tools and did some improvement events. Jim was excited about the ideas and initial results, but sustaining those improvements always seemed beyond the organization's grasp. "We just couldn't make it stick," Jim says.

Then he moved up to lead a larger hospital in Muscatine, Iowa, in 2009 and plunged into the work of turning around a troubled facility. UnityPoint Health–Trinity Muscatine has a total of 80 inpatient beds and 450 employees in a small town nestled in a big bend in the Mississippi River. The organization has about 1,800 inpatient admissions annually; physicians handle 120,000 clinic visits. It did not have an effective continuous improvement program.

The very first step Jim took on returning from his visit to Wisconsin with several other hospital leaders was to call together the physicians, all of whom are employed by UnityPoint Health. Jim described lean and the business performance system he had seen. "I told them that what we saw was the future of healthcare. It would be a lot of work, and we couldn't do it halfway. So, I asked whether they were in agreement to do this," Jim said. "Then one of the surgeons who went to ThedaCare stood up and said it wasn't a matter of *if* we should do it but how fast we could get going."

Next, Jim went to the hospital's board of directors to solicit support for lean and the new business management system. It was an easy sell, Jim says, since most of the board members were local business leaders who used lean thinking to some degree in their own companies. But he was asking for more than simple agreement.

"I asked for a commitment from the board that not only would they support creation of a lean management system but also if I left or retired, they would search for a replacement CEO with lean as a core competency," Jim told me. "I didn't want this to be my pet project. I wanted it to become the way we think and do business at Trinity Muscatine."

When the board agreed, Jim got to work creating a launch plan. He knew that he did not want any kaizen or rapid improvement events at the hospital until the new management structure was in place. So, Jim hired a consultant, and together they established a 16-week training course for senior staff on the "nuts and bolts" of lean, integrated with what they called the Trinity Muscatine business management system. For two days a week, eight hours each day, over the course of three months the team, including all six members of senior staff and three senior managers or directors, learned A3 thinking, standard work, value-stream mapping, observation, mentoring and coaching, and other skills. It was a huge time commitment for the entire senior staff to be engaged like that while still running a hospital, but they were committed.

Next, Jim and his senior staff identified four pilot departments, based on the enthusiasm of area managers, and began passing on what they had learned. Nutrition, radiology, medical/surgical, and an outpatient pediatric clinic learned to use stat sheets, huddle boards, and problem solving with an A3. Senior staff did the training, supported by consultants, and spent a lot of time observing and mentoring those first units.

Less than a year later, another six departments went through training, erected huddle boards, and began having stat sheet conversations and tracking metrics. Meanwhile, the first four pilot units received more training and incorporated more components in their work, including standard work observations, leadership advisory teams, and monthly scorecard meetings. After two years, in 2014, this regional hospital will have finished the initial phase of its lean management conversion, Jim says, with all units trained in most or all of the components and working to incorporate the work into their daily routines.

Leadership at Muscatine is also experimenting with different ways to handle scorecards. In late 2013, they had a monthly scorecard of financial indicators that was reported to the board, as well as a quarterly quality scorecard. The senior team also selected 11 watch indicators that they believe show the health of the organization. These are reported and discussed weekly, and, if an indicator falls outside of the expected limits, the senior team begins an A3 to analyze and correct the problem.

If Jim had to do it all over again, he told me, the one thing he would do differently is communicate the vision a little better. He would have set out a clear schedule of training and let everyone know that every department would be switching to the new business management system by a particular date. Too many people became anxious about the special attention being given the pilot units, Jim says, and then Trinity Muscatine began to seem a little bipolar. There were problem solvers on one side and firefighters on the other. When they needed departments to work together for patients, the two mind-sets sometimes had a hard time communicating.

If he was allowed to implement only one aspect of a lean management system, Jim says, he would use stat sheets. Staff members talking to their managers every day about the problems that may arise and thinking proactively instead of reacting has created the most positive change he has seen. Of course, nobody should implement stat sheets alone. Once we identify problems, we need to offer people a way to work through those problems scientifically and fix the issues. Jim agrees and says that A3 education would be his close second choice for a favorite element.

"Really, the best thing about all of this is seeing people get fired up," Jim says. "When the light comes on and they see the benefit to their work or to their patients, they get really excited. Our conversations around here have changed dramatically."

## Providence Little Company of Mary: California

When Mary Kingston arrived in Torrance, California, in 2011 as the new chief operating officer of the 450-bed hospital, she knew the learning curve would be steep. The lean healthcare initiative at Providence Little Company of Mary (PLCOM) was limited to two lean/Six Sigma facilitators who ran projects. They were good facilitators but had a hard time engaging hospital employees using project-based methods. Most of the 2,000+ employees of this busy Los Angeles County beach city hospital were unfamiliar with lean thinking and tools.

Previously, Mary had been actively involved in the lean transformation at the large St. Joseph's Health system that stretches from Texas to Oregon.

While there, she had studied with a variety of lean thinkers and had begun implementing the elements of our business performance system. She knew how far PLCOM had to go. The question was, would the organization be willing?

CEO Liz Dunne had been instrumental in bringing lean thinking to her previous medical center, too, so she was interested in the idea of a lean management system and green-lighted Mary's plans. From there, Mary's very first move was perhaps the easiest and yet most courageous: she took all of her direct reports and went to gemba.

At first, it was just Mary and her group of eight, including the chief nursing officer; the directors of emergency, surgery, case management, support services, and specialty services such as radiation oncology; the manager of clinical nutrition services; and the director of the laboratory, blood bank, and pathology. Every day, they would walk through the hallways, checking in with clinicians and technicians on the unit and talking about how to identify the issues that could affect patient care. Then, Mary developed a "rounding report" so they could capture what they were seeing every day—the wasted time and motion, the safety issues, the lack of coordination.

From there, it was an easy leap to stat sheets or, as they are called in this hospital, direct-report trackers. Everyone at PLCOM just calls them "trackers" now, but it still means the daily scripted questions that ulti-mately tie to the organization's strategic initiatives. To introduce the idea, Mary began working through the daily scripted conversation with a few of her direct reports who seemed most interested in the idea. "I started doing trackers early on because I was new to the organization and wanted to learn about my direct reports," Mary says. "Trackers gave me a structured way to do it."

The next step, which followed very quickly on the first, was to send directors and managers through a green-belt training course. Although "belt training" is borrowed from Six Sigma nomenclature, the course was not about searching for statistical indications of process deviations. This training focused on teaching managers basic lean tools, how to identify problems, how to work through A3s, and how to mentor problem solvers. The course included two weeks of intense classroom training interspersed with two workshops on change management and facilitation. Trainees also needed to complete two projects approved by executives and the operational excellence manager and pass a written test before calling themselves green belts.

There were 70 managers, directors, and supervisors to train, so the leadership team put together small cohorts of 10 or 15 people to go through training together and scheduled three full training sessions within the first 18 months. By the end of 2013, Mary says, two-thirds of leaders had been trained, and she thought training would be complete within the following year.

Next, they set up direct-report trackers and department-based huddle boards everywhere and started teaching and coaching staff members in the new protocols they call their leadership development system. As at ThedaCare, Mary's own direct-report tracker has content that cascades downward—with some variation, of course—to the trackers of managers and supervisors. Mary's direct reports lead the daily huddles. Team members typically gather around huddle boards at shift change or early in the shift as the staff prepares to hand off patients and work. The discussions are clinical as well as improvement focused and may include ideas from other units, since every unit has a hospital-wide communication board set up nearby. This executive communication board details the results of projects in other areas and spreads information from other huddles, as well as from patient-safety rounds. In this way, Mary achieves two things: cross-germination of improvement ideas and a consistent, subtle reminder of the support that the leadership development system has from the top at this hospital.

The huddle board has proved so useful that many units have created individual huddle boards for every patient bedside. This is where patient condition, special notes and restrictions, vital signs, care plans, goals, and expected release dates are all noted. Clinicians can meet with each other and family members at the board to discuss care and ensure that important notes, such as fall risks, pain status, and questions for physicians, are there for everyone to see.

To ensure accountability, Mary also began conducting weekly "management flash" meetings to review progress of metrics, weekly operational improvement meetings to review metric progress in greater detail, and a monthly operating review meeting. This is similar to a monthly scorecard meeting with weekly updates.

Once the initial groups were trained and units were up and running on continuous improvement with huddles and trackers, momentum began to build quickly. Physicians asked when lean improvements would come to their departments. Board members toured departments that were doing the work and asked questions. The executive team celebrated units that were making great strides and was sometimes astonished at how quickly units took to the new system.

In the emergency department, for instance, teams of doctors, nurses, and administrators used A3 thinking and huddles to figure out a new way to slash waiting time that is worth sharing. An E.D. improvement team collected data on how long people were waiting for treatment and then grouped people by severity of trauma, from one (severe) to five (minor). What they found was a spike in waiting time for levels four and five. These are the patients who are not in immediate danger and have mostly self-diagnosed their trouble. They need a few stitches, have a fractured wrist, or are dizzy with no other symptoms. Level four and five patients could wait in the E.D. for six hours before seeing a doctor simply because sicker patients needed to be seen first. And there's nothing like a six-hour wait to drive down your customer satisfaction.

The E.D. improvement teams at PLCOM found they could "super track" these patients and make a huge difference in wait times. By creating a separate care system for the ambulatory, nonserious cases with a dedicated clinical staff and separate seating area, they could ensure that the E.D. waiting room was less clogged while these less severe cases were seen in a timely fashion. Another process improvement ensured that any necessary laboratory or other diagnostic work was completed by the time these patients met with a physician.

"A physician from the E.D. stopped me recently, about 11 months after we began working there, and told me that the work was going so well it felt like they had been using lean thinking and the leadership development system for years," Mary says. "The people there are already different. They are more courageous about confronting issues and less tolerant of seeing the same problems over and over again."

If Mary could do it over again with one change, she says, she would have been more deliberate about resource planning. Those lean facilitators already working in the hospital should have been deployed into the huddles for real-time coaching. When so many people are starting a new system together, it is important to identify your experts and send them out to where novices are practicing, Mary says.

After two years of internal transformation—with bigger and more significant changes coming at the hospital fast as a result of changes in healthcare law—Mary says the best aspect of lean and leadership development at PLCOM in Torrance can be summed up in a single word: preparedness. Operations have become more efficient and financially stable, Mary says. More important, leaders and staff have been creating a culture that is more adaptable. And that flexibility is going to come in handy as the healthcare industry faces unprecedented change.

"What if we need to de-license the entire fourth floor of the hospital because the rules have changed and now all the patients in those beds fall into the outpatient category?" Mary says. "Two years ago, I think everyone would have freaked out about that possibility. Now, they know how to think through big changes in a very deliberative fashion. I know that I'm a better leader for going through this and all of us are better prepared."

## Hospital for Sick Children: Ontario, Canada

Jeff Mainland knows something about managing change; he has had plenty in his career. With a background in nuclear medicine and then forensic pathology, he spent years performing autopsies for the chief coroner in Ontario, Canada, and then became chief of staff for Parliament's Minister of Education before joining the staff of the Hospital for Sick Children, affectionately known as SickKids, as director of strategic projects. His résumé can give you whiplash.

At this 300-bed hospital—Canada's largest pediatric academic health center—that treats 15,000 inpatient children every year and another 300,000 in 100 outpatient clinics, Jeff has led the efforts to implement a Balanced Scorecard system of strategic alignment and execution. And he coleads a partnership effort with the Hamad Medical Corporation to build a 200+ bed pediatric hospital in Doha, Qatar. He does not lack energy. And yet, he was having a hard time getting continuous improvement work to expand beyond the laboratory, where individual projects had resulted in discrete improvements.

Then in 2011, SickKids joined a government-sponsored initiative to improve processes in emergency departments around Ontario. Involvement got them a lean coach who told Jeff to go take a look at ThedaCare.

Now executive vice president for strategy, quality, performance, and communications, Jeff went straight to the CEO of SickKids to pitch the business performance system when he returned to Toronto. Mary Jo Haddad was interested and asked Jeff to draw up a business plan for a lean transformation. In the plan, Jeff included four new employees—all lean experts from outside healthcare—to create internal expertise and provide expert coaching.

Preferring to go an inch wide and a mile deep while implementing the new program that the leadership team called Daily CIP (continuous improvement program), they chose two pilot areas on which to focus. The neurosurgery unit and a general medicine unit both had managers with track records of successfully implementing new programs and were willing to do so again.

"One of the biggest challenges is to cascade a strategy deeply into a complex organization so that it is meaningful to frontline employees," Jeff says. "'Champion continuous improvement' has been an annual objective since 2010, but nothing significant happened. Now, I saw the vehicle to make it happen while keeping the organization aligned to our strategic direction. I really wanted this."

The Daily CIP teams made a lot of changes very quickly in those two clinical units, by training and implementing all eight components of the business performance system. Very soon, Jeff was getting inquiries from several other units interested in starting their own huddles or stat sheets. But Jeff and his team decided to keep doing full implementations on each new unit instead of training individual components piecemeal.

They set up a curriculum and training schedule for units that put them through in waves of four or five at a time.[52]

"After that first wave went through, we had to put chains on the gates. I had managers of other units asking me to just get them started on huddle boards or status sheets right away. They saw the engagement level and performance improvements on the pilot units and wanted it," Jeff says. "But we really believe that you can't improve performance in a sustainable way with just one element like a status sheet. For those to work, you need the huddle boards and visual management and the structured problem solving you get from working through PDSAs."

For all the enthusiasm, Jeff says, teams at SickKids have also struggled. Deciding what to measure and getting fast, accurate data had not been easy. Many units had different requirements and the hospital's 10-person decision support unit was largely a manual operation. In late 2013, they were beginning the automation process, pulling together a lot of individual databases and building an integrated performance measurement system. By then, Jeff knew what they needed. "I don't want just numbers," he says. "I want the intelligence that data give us."

Daily CIP has changed SickKids in more ways than new measurements and huddle boards, of course. The real point of all this work can best be seen in two places: hand hygiene compliance and medication reconciliation.

Hand hygiene compliance has been a safety and quality problem in healthcare from the very beginning. SickKids had been working on improving compliance for more than a decade without any great breakthroughs. Once they put the issue on the status sheet, though, causing dozens of people to address the issue every day, the needle started

---

52. In January 2014, the final four inpatient units underwent training and the Daily CIP transformation. The rollout in all inpatient units required about two years.

to move. In the 18 months following their April 2012 inclusion of hand hygiene on stat sheets, compliance rates moved from 70% to 82%.

Medication reconciliation metrics benefited from stat sheet conversations, too, as well as from visual management creating a drive for improvement on the unit level. At SickKids, they measure medication reconciliation by how many patients go through a full reconciliation process on entering, transferring within the hospital, and leaving the hospital. After focusing their efforts for one full year on the medication reconciliation process with stat sheets, huddle boards, and scorecards throughout the hospital, they were halfway to 100% perfect. In August 2012, just 66% of patients[53] had their medications completely reconciled. In March 2012, it was 74% and in August 2013, it was 83%.

"We were never even close to 80% before. It was an amazing turn-around," Jeff says.

## New York City Health and Hospitals Corporation

Joanna Omi's problems were the same as everyone else's, really. The senior vice president of organizational innovation and effectiveness at the New York City Health and Hospitals Corporation (HHC), she struggled with sustaining lean-based improvements. She knew that lean knowledge needed to deeply penetrate the organization and wanted to better engage staff in continuous improvement. The only difference at HHC was one of scale.

The largest municipal health system in the United States, HHC serves 1.4 million patients annually in 11 acute-care hospitals and more than 70 community health centers. A $6.7-billion budget includes 35,000 employees.

---

53. This measures patients who were transferred to other facilities.

In late 2007, HHC began an enterprise-wide lean transformation that they call Breakthrough. By June 2012, Joanna was overseeing an effort that included 60 lean facilitators and Breakthrough deployment officers utilized throughout HHC and could claim $343 million in combined savings and new revenue. It was impressive, but the leadership team at HHC was not content.

"We had done 1,000 or more rapid improvement events, and our sustainment rates were not what they should be. We were cycling some of the same people through training and events each time," Joanna says. "So we weren't reaching deeply enough into the organization. We needed a stronger infrastructure."

So, Joanna started asking around for who was doing well with continuous improvement and started traveling. She went to Harvard Vanguard Medical Associates in Massachusetts and ThedaCare in Wisconsin; she went to manufacturers such as Ford Motor Company's River Rouge plant in Michigan, Wiremold in Connecticut, and HID, the company that makes HHC's identification badges.

"There was a lot of variety in the way people innovated, but a few things were the same," Joanna says. "I saw highly visual processes and lots of management alignment, allowing for successive levels of the organization to see the same information and react to it. And people needed to touch something—to take notes or go look or collect data—in order to interact with the system."

With about 2,000 managers throughout HHC representing a variety of skills and business sophistication, Joanna knew that training them to perform in a similar fashion would be key. She pulled together a team and spent months developing manager training, only to judge it inadequate. "Helping managers accomplish their work in a new way would require much more practical application than classroom time," Joanna says.

"Most of us have been rewarded for our ability to get through crises, to tend to urgent needs. But today's work requires a different way of thinking and behaving. We needed to help them get to *predictable*, to find root causes. They needed lean basics."

Joanna also needed their input on how to design the system and training, she decided. So she pulled together 40 people from throughout the organization in dyads—one person from operations linked with one lean facilitator, representing all of the larger sites and subsidiaries—for a presentation on the business performance system. Then she asked the dyads to go think about how this system might best work at HHC and run experiments at their home sites. What would be most useful? How could they keep it linked to operational strategy? "You are the champions of change," she told them. "What you do will form the basis for what we create throughout the system. Test the components, play around with it, and let's talk again in a few months."

About half the original group came back with significant findings and offered reports on their experiments in perioperative services, primary care, and outpatient mental health services. This feedback on what worked and what was needed in order to make it succeed was invaluable.

With this input, Joanna put together a team that weighed one of the questions that confronts all large organizations: can both depth and breadth be achieved in the rollout of a new management system, or would one have to be sacrificed? They knew time would be an issue because nobody had enough of it. They could not introduce a half-formed management system. So they constructed a model of the system and its rollout on paper, covering one large wall, and then Joanna got more input on that from HHC leadership, lean staff, and managers. Then a smaller team put together the final model for their daily management system based on the plan and input.

The rollout was in phases, beginning with four pilot sites in four different facilities. Each of the four site CEOs supported the work with regular gemba walks, and a senior manager acted as the daily management system champion. The champion received onsite coaching as he or she worked with staff to create huddle boards and process control boards. Coaching and training for these pilot sites were provided by internal and external lean coaches, who provided continuous support for the initial week and then tapered back as needed.

Local managers owned the area huddle boards and learned how and what to measure in order to achieve improvements. They received coaching on how to give progress reports—"daily briefs"—at the board. Instead of using stat sheets to engage staff, the area manager assigned people on a rotating basis to follow one of five True North metrics. These people were responsible for reviewing current conditions surrounding their metric every day, updating the DMS board in time for the huddle, and then taking turns to brief their colleagues in a stand-up report at the board.

In phase two, those same four pilot sites received further training in using the scientific method to problem solve and incorporated that into their daily management system improvement efforts. Standard work for leaders, including gemba walks and participation in tiered briefs, as well as kamishibai auditing, was also added in this phase. Phase three will include standard work for senior executives.

Meanwhile, new sites are being launched on a steady schedule. At the end of 2013, there were 15 areas in eight sites practicing the daily management system. Joanna's target is to be up and running in 244 sites by the end of 2015. Senior executives are counting on a certain amount of viral enthusiasm and the learn-do-teach model of training to get that done.

Why does Joanna think enthusiasm for the program might make it viral? HHC has already seen a significant jump in patient satisfaction scores in the sites that have adopted daily management. It turns out that staff members like being asked for their opinion. They like addressing entrenched, long-standing problems and making a difference. In turn, they present a more optimistic face to patients.

"And we're cleaning up the mess! We are reducing wait times; people are seeing their own doctors quickly. We are working better together," Joanna says. "Patient satisfaction scores are going up. It scares me to even say that out loud, but the numbers prove it."

About one year into the rollout, Joanna says that her favorite outcome so far has been the level of ownership she's seen in the early sites. The huddle board becomes fully owned and maintained by the unit within weeks of installation. Within months, she invariably hears from adjacent sites or units working in the same value stream, inquiring about when they will get a board. These are New Yorkers, after all, and they do not like to wait.

## Conclusion

It has been exciting for me to see how each organization has personalized the system and adapted ideas to fit its own culture. This is exactly what we were hoping for when we began teaching the business performance system as individual components. We wanted it to be adaptable, scalable, and flexible. These organizations and leaders are proving that it is.

What is most striking when I look at the experiences of these organizations, however, is the linkage—the magnetism, if you will— between the components of this system. The hospitals that began quickly with stat sheets only or stat sheets and huddle boards found themselves implementing and teaching visual management and leader standard work before they knew it. If you erect a huddle board and post your objectives and progress, after all, you are practicing transparency. If a manager shows up every day to have a stat sheet conversation and then lead a huddle, that manager is practicing standard work—as are the executives who meet to review their scorecards. It might not be perfectly realized in the beginning and it might not be very robust, but the practice has begun.

When you unpack a business performance system, it turns out to be like a barrel of monkeys. One component grabs another and drags it out onto the gemba. Stat sheets are standard work. Huddle boards are transparency. Stat sheets and huddles both need A3 problem solving to work through issues. Problem solving requires standard work. (There can be no sustainable improvement without standardization.) Standard work needs observation at gemba to save it from drift. And all leaders need scorecards to remain clear about their actual performance—whether they are improving and whether problem solving results in real improvement over time. Focus on the linkages between the components and it is easy to see how each piece is also the whole.

Still, readers might have questions. In particular, you may be wondering about the results of this experiment. What have we really accomplished at ThedaCare since that summer of 2008, and have we moved the needle on our metrics? I went back and looked at our metrics since 2006 and found that the answer is not simple. We do not have a single metric that exists in the same form year over year, so tracking just one thing over time is not possible. We have, however, tracked the results of individual units and clinics as they adopted the business performance system and began keeping metrics. Significant improvements are clearly seen in these areas. This is not easily translatable to our True North metrics, however, particularly since our appetite for aggressive goals also increased and hitting annual targets became markedly more difficult.

Let's see what we do have. It was very important to us that we validated the effectiveness of the business performance system in those early days before we spread the work through the hospitals and the system, so we painstakingly tracked those improvement data. The alpha cohort—our first experiments in 2009—involved five units: inpatient oncology, a radiation oncology clinic, and three medical surgical units. The metrics below reflect the difference between baseline data taken in 2008 and after implementation of the business performance system in 2009. Here are the results:

- All five units improved between 9% and 68% on the quality drivers (patient falls, Coumadin education, pain assessment, delays in access, and interactions with patients within 1 day of discharge).

- Three of the five units improved 3%–48% on the employee engagement index. One unit showed no change and one unit showed a 1% decline from a previously high score.

- All five units improved 1%–11% in financial stewardship as measured by productivity improvement (clinical labor costs/unit of service).

In 2010, as we spread the business performance system to our beta group, we experienced similar results.

- Quality drivers improved in 14 of the 17 beta units (88%).

- Employee engagement scores improved from 4 % to 10% in every unit except one over the prior year. It is important to note that one unit actually decreased 10% in employee engagement; we attributed this to significant disruptions, such as staffing model changes, at the time of the assessment.

- When we reviewed customer satisfaction drivers, 85% (11 out of 13) of the units improved.

- The final metric of financial stewardship demonstrated that 48% (12 of 23) of the units improved by more than 3.1% productivity improvement over the prior year.

Our final formal assessment of improvement metrics occurred in 2011.

- 80% of the people metrics improved (4 of 5 unit drivers).

- 77% of the quality metrics improved (37 of 48 unit drivers).

- 78% of the financial stewardship metrics improved (57 of 73 unit drivers).

After this final validation, we spread the business performance system beyond the experimental cells, all through the hospital division, and later to the rest of the ThedaCare system.

Today we measure our performance through our True North metric review. Our current metrics all have percentage targets beyond general improvement. They are aggressive and consistently target a baseline improvement that exceeds the prior year's progress.

Our goal is to develop our people, solve problems, and improve performance. This is hard work. We never feel like we are doing well enough. We see problems and defects everywhere, and we continue to struggle to meet our goals. I wish I could say we have arrived at perfection, but that is far from the truth. Our strength is that we know that daily improvement is a major part of our overall lean strategy and we have a plan to make it happen. Each day we strive to perform better than yesterday.

As you begin your journey to better management, you will find that perseverance is required as well as humility. The lean toolbox is rich and we need all of the tools, starting with A3 thinking, value-stream mapping, and team-based kaizen improvements. The business performance system is simply another set of tools to help us continuously improve and sustain the gains. It is not magic, but it may be the real work that has been missing in healthcare.

Still, complaints about the new system will be common in some quarters. It will take perseverance to keep those who are entrenched in traditional management models from overthrowing the movement. Also, you will have failures. I hope that yours are less frequent than mine were, and I hope you find the humility to accept failures, pick yourself up, and try again. In the end, you are doing this for your organization's leadership, to enable them to better help your patients, and they desperately need it.

So this is my final word: start somewhere. Take the first step and work through it diligently while listening to and developing your people. Each component will follow on the heels of the next. Whether you begin with two components across your organization or, like Jeff Mainland, start with all components in two pilot sites, the important thing is to begin.

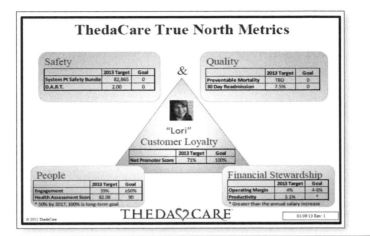

| Measure of | ThedaCare True North Metrics |
|---|---|
| Safety | **System Patient Safety Bundle**<br>Increase flu vaccine rate, increase pneumonia vaccine rate,<br>increase medication reconsolidation, reduce patient falls, and reduce MRSA |
| Safety | **D.A.R.T.**<br>Employee injuries and illness as measured by<br>Days Away, Restricted or Transferred (D.A.R.T.) rate |
| Quality | **Preventable Mortality**<br>Non end-of-life patient deaths that occur while under our care that,<br>if treated optimally, would have been prevented |
| Quality | **30-Day Readmission Rate**<br>Rate of AMC or TCMC hospital patients that had an inpatient stay and were<br>readmitted back to any of our five hospitals within 30 days for any reason |
| Customer Satisfaction | **Customer Loyalty**<br>Net promoter score - likelihood for a patient to recommend us to friends or family |
| People | **Employee Engagement Index**<br>Measured by the employee engagement survey |
| People | **H.A.T. Scores**<br>Employee health as measured by the health assessment tool |
| Financial Stewardship | **Operating Margin**<br>Revenue in excess of expenses as calculated by system revenue divided by expenses |
| Financial Stewardship | **Productivity**<br>Productivity as calculated by deflated gross revenue (revenue less than value<br>of price increases) divided by hours worked at the system level |

ThedaCare True North Metrics

# Acknowledgments

As journeys go, this has been challenging and rewarding. We learned from many people in other industries that blazed the lean path before us. We read, we practiced, and we developed a plan. We took one step at a time and created a system that we believed might work for us. Our leadership was courageous and committed. For that I am so grateful. We were ready for something to help us navigate the changes necessary to achieve the new management vision. So my first acknowledgment must recognize our compass. We depended on our sensei Jose Bustillo to keep us on course and challenge our direction. His support and guidance made the vision real; our teams made the achievement possible.

We developed a team of vulnerable, courageous, and very flexible leaders who experimented with and improved the elements of our business performance system. That first team we called our developmental lab, and it included MaryJeanne Schaffmeyer, Karen Flom, Shawn Chartier, and Patsy Engel. They have influenced and helped to shape this work from conception. I also need to thank Kathryn Correia for creating the space in our work for this team and those that followed to learn and grow.

Additionally, I want to recognize the many members of the steering committee for their tireless and dedicated work and the unit leaders who brought this work to life. This team was a true collaboration between our Human Development Value Stream, the ThedaCare Improvement System (lean office), and the hospital leadership team all working together to give breath to the business performance system.

You will notice that I did not write this book alone. You will see this work from many different voices and I want to acknowledge how important their work was in influencing and shaping key aspects of this book by bringing its intentions to life. Shawn Chartier, Shana Herzfeldt,

Pam Malkowski, Michael Vela, Karen Flom, Vicki Van Epps, Patsy Engel, MaryJeanne Schaffmeyer, Jodi Braun, Michael Radke, Jennifer Fredriksen, Jill Menzel, Debra VandenLangenberg, Jill Case-Wirth, Dan Collins, Gina Moon, Jill Perrett, James McGovern, Clark Boren, and Mark Hermans were all crucial to this work. Shawn, Shana, and Mike Radke also cheerfully acquiesced to posing for the book's cover and for that, I'm grateful.

I want to also thank the leaders from other parts of North America for letting us share their success with our readers: Mary Kingston, chief operating officer, Providence Little Company of Mary in Torrance, California; Joanna Omi, senior vice president of organizational innovation and effectiveness at the New York City Health and Hospitals Corporation; Jim Hayes, chief executive officer, Unity Point Health–Trinity Muscatine, Iowa; and Jeff Mainland, executive vice president for strategy, quality, performance, and communications, Hospital for Sick Children, Ontario, Canada.

The success of many of us has been supported by external consultant groups. Three groups have helped with the work identified in this text. I want to call them out by name and thank them for their support and leadership: Jose Bustillo with Simpler Consulting; KPMG, led by Gordon Burrill; and Value Capture, led by Ken Segel.

I want to thank Dean Gruner, ThedaCare's CEO, for his encouragement and support of our lean journey, as well as all of our senior leadership team for their courage and support.

There are so many others who have added their valuable insights and who have made us better because of their work. I wish I could mention them each by name.

Jim Womack and John Toussaint paved the path for this book—without their gentle and not-so-gentle nudging, editing, and encouragement, this body of work would not be as rich. Thank you for your time, thoughtful reflection, and belief in the work. I would never have taken this writing journey without you. Also, thanks to Helen Zak and Steve Bollinger from the ThedaCare Center for Healthcare Value, who took care of the thousand details involved in publishing a book.

Emily Adams made my words and thoughts come to life and improved every aspect of this work. You spoke from my heart. Thank you.

Thank you to my children, Jereme, Caleb, and Sarah, for your love and encouragement.

And, last, a thank-you to my inspiration, John Utrie, D.O. You encouraged me and sustained my soul with your absolute belief in me. Your insight made this work better.

# Appendix

To download the graphics from *Beyond Heroes*, visit createvalue.org/
beyondheroes

Type in the passcode: TrueNorth

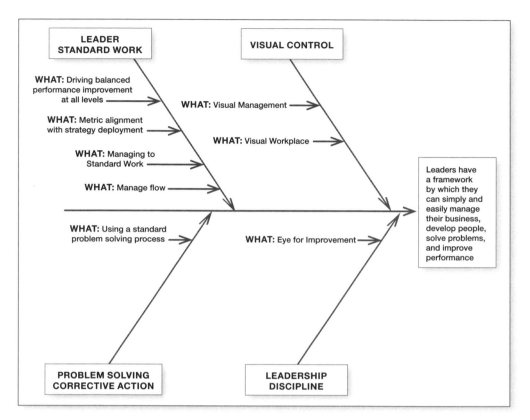

Figure 1. Reverse Fishbone Diagram

Success statement: Leaders have a framework by which they can simply and easily manage their business, develop people, solve problems, and improve performance.

## Leader Standard Work:

**What:** Driving balanced performance improvement at all levels
 How: Shift huddles
      Daily performance and defect review
      Weekly planning
      Monthly performance review
      Business rules around WIP
      Countermeasure reports when metrics are red

**What:** Metric alignment with strategy deployment
 How: Strategic policy deployment
      Information flow map
      Production control, tally sheet, spreadsheet, scorecard
      Annual strategic planning
      Simple metric management tool
      Alignment with DR re: data mgmt/ reporting

**What:** Managing to Standard Work
 How: Create daily standard work for structure of day
      Standard work in place and visual
      Standard work for gemba: daily, weekly
      Leader audits for standard work, visual management, 6S
      Process to review/ update standard work
      Document management system for standard work

**What:** Manage flow
 How: Create flow cells
      Consider organizational structure with cells
      Manage to standard work

## Visual Control:

**What:** Visual Management

  How:  Standard work for boards and lanes (evidence of problem solving and corrective action)

  Appropriate frequency of performance tracking (hourly, daily, consider pitch)

  Graphical depiction of performance over time

  Scorecard for snapshot view of metrics

  Metric alignment posted (SD,VS, daily)

  Plan/ Activities posted

**What:** Visual Workplace:

  How:  Standard work for visual management

  6S

  Andon's in-work location

  Working knowledge of demand (daily, weekly, monthly, annually)

  Data management and analysis skills

## Problem Solving and Corrective Action:

**What:** Using a standard problem solving process

  How:  Standard work defined with a defined outcome or specification (so I know it is done correctly)

  Use of tools in area (SW sheet, SW combo, key points, labor bar chart)

  Make problem visual (true transparency of defects and opportunities )

  Timely responding / solving problems

  Detection and prevention of defects

  Containment

  Root-cause analysis

Implement countermeasures

Verify if you have correct root cause or countermeasure

Escalation standard work for flow stoppers/ defects

Problem solving and corrective action evident (hourly, daily, monthly)

## Leadership Discipline:

**What:**  Eye for improvement

Build a team

Clear expectations and accountability at all levels

Managing staffing to demand

On the job development

Leaders are "in the work"

Teach others

Coaching and reinforcement

Willingness to learn/ coachability

Evidence of application of PDSA

Demonstrated daily problem solving

Rigorous mentoring program (everyone has a coach)

Alignment in activity vs. priorities

Manage operational change

How:  To be determined by Human Development Value Stream.

Scope of work

PDP / competencies

Job descriptions and functions

Skills matrix

Portfolio requirements

Curriculum for leadership development

Certification process

| Title: | BPS-Phase II | Fresh Eyes: | |
|---|---|---|---|
| Owner: | Kim Barnas /Patsy Engel | Team: | Hospital Leadership Team |
| PDSA Coach: | Jose Bustillo, Brian Preston | | |

**Background / Current Conditions**

In May of 2008 the Business Performance System was developed in response to the following problem statement:
**We are on a continuous improvement cultural transformation and current systems for managing the business are not in alignment with new expectations. Leaders at ThedaCare have their own way to manage their business. Leaders do not know their performance. There is high variability to how we approach and respond to problems.**

**Original Vision Statement:** Develop a business Management System that frees leaders to transform their business while profoundly affecting the lives of our patients and staff through developing people to solve problems to improve performance.

The development and implementation of BPs was done as an experiment in the hospital division.
BPS was founded on 5 foundational elements: Leader Standard Work, Visual Control, Problem Solving and Corrective Action, Leadership Development, Leadership Discipline.
•The original hypothesis was that with the development of BPS managers would have clear performance expectations, clear role and management expectations, and a balanced approach to leadership development. Attributes of the Target state included:
- **Managers knowing their performance**
- **Disciplined adherence to BPS leadership standard work**
- **Production control boards to know hour by hour at the gemba**
- **Tracking centers to know day by day and month by month**
- **Scheduled standardized performance review meetings**
- **Information used to control process and results**
- **Consistent performance improvement over time**
- **Organizational structure**
- **Standard work at all levels for leaders**
- **Know how to manage to standard work**

The above attributes have been largely achieved in the hospital division with the implementation of BPS(achieved in red) . Currently 91% of hospital managers have been trained and are practicing the elements of BPS. The following results have been achieved in the areas of quality, safety, employee engagement, and financial stewardship.

*Business Performance System Timeline*

| Quality | Accidents | | Decrease 50% by 6/2010 | 2009-Decrease in hospital fall rate 51% with sustainment in 2010 |
|---|---|---|---|---|
| | | | | 2010-AMC/TC Reportable Incident rate (sprains and strains) reduced 17.4% |
| Business | | | Increase by 0% by 6/2010 | 2009 Alpha Units 1-11% productivity increase |
| | Productivity | | | 2010 Productivity target not met |
| Employee Engagement | % managers practicing BPS | | TBD | Year end 2009-61% |
| | | | | Year end 2010-91% |
| Employee Engagement | # times mgr interacts with staff in problem solving | | TBD | Daily in performance review huddle |
| Employee Engagement | # of improvement ideas per unit | | 300 per unit/yr | Average 285 per unit 2010 |

*2010 BPS Scorecard Driver Improvement*
*True North Driver Category*

*BPS Alpha Units-Percent Employees "Engaged"*

*AMC BPS Beta Units-Employees "Engaged"*
*ThedaClark BPS Beta Units-Employees "Engaged"*

Although the above achievements have supported the original hypothesis, the current BPS product has not yielded consistent , significant ,continuous Improvement in the area of productivity . In 2010 the nursing units at AMC and TC had an overall increase in clinical prod hours of 5.1% and an increase in clinical labor costs of 7.1% (after wage adjustment) from 2009. The clinical hour increase resulted in $1.02 million of the total $2.3 million in increased staffing costs.
It has also been noted throughout the division that there has been little emphasis on managing to standard work in order to sustain improvement and continue improving.

| Overall Metrics | Measure | Initial | Target |
|---|---|---|---|
| Quality | | | |
| Business | | | |
| | Productivity | 0 | % of BPS units with 3.5% improvement |
| Employee Engagement | % hospital managers practicing BPS | 91% | 100% |
| Employee Engagement | # of improvement ideas per unit | 285 (avg /unit) | 300 per unit/yr |

**Executive**
•Strategy
•Market Share
•Modeling the Way
•Innovation
•Developing People

**Manager /Supervisor**
•Goals
•Daily Operations
•Flow
•Developing People
•Solving Problems

**Staff**
•Tactical
•Problem Solving

©20 3

Figure 2. A3 Business Performance System

| Subject | Hospital managers/HLT | Start Date: | 5/2008 original |
| --- | --- | --- | --- |
| Expert(s): | | Revision Date: | 5/16/2011 |
| | | Revision #: | 4 |

## PLAN

**Analysis / Root Cause/ Countermeasures (potential solutions)**

| Key Problems | Root Cause |
| --- | --- |
| 1. Productivity improvements not met in 2011 | We have not imbedded a consistent systematic process for removing waste from unit process flows so we have been unable to reduce FTE |
| 2. Improvements made through projects, RIEs etc. have not been sustained consistently | There has been little emphasis or consistency in training to standard, observing standard, or coaching to standard. |
| 3. Through observation it appears that there is a lack competency and comfort in real time coaching around standard work | This is a new skill being required of leaders |
| 4. Only 91% of Hospital Managers trained in BPS | Have added some new managers with ACA, and role changes Have not had capacity in past cohorts to include facilities, medical records, food service. |

## DO

**Experiments to Root Causes**

| Key Problems | Root Cause | Solution Approach /Experiments |
| --- | --- | --- |
| 1. Productivity improvements not met in 2011 | We have not embedded a consistent systematic process for removing waste from unit process flows so we have been unable to reduce FTE | Experiments underway in 2 units on flowing and removing waste |
| 2. Improvements made through projects, RIEs etc. have not been sustained consistently | There has been little emphasis or consistency in training to standard, observing standard, or coaching to standard | Training on Process observation done 1/2011 Process observation implemented by 22/29 BPS managers Training on Training to Standard Work 5/11 Experiment with IV med administration team on training and observation |
| 3. Through observation it appears that there is a lack competency and comfort in real time coaching around standard work | This is a new skill being required of leaders | Involve OD in becoming experiment in their work around this competency Kim and Patsy training on Just Culture 4/5/2011 Will be involved in further work on integrating Just Culture into training and coaching. |
| 4. Only 91% of Hospital Managers trained in BPS | Have added some new managers with ACA, and role changes Have not had capacity in past cohorts to include facilities, medical records, food service. | Additional cohort to begin 8/15/11 to train additional managers. |

## STUDY

**Study (Planned vs. Actual Results)**

| Overall Metrics | Measure | Initial | Target | Date Achieved |
| --- | --- | --- | --- | --- |
| **Quality** | | | | |
| **Business** | Productivity | | % of BPS units with 3.5% Improvement | Note: May 2011 65% of managers at target for month |
| Employee Engagement | % hospital managers practicing BPS | 91% | 100% | 91% |
| Employee Engagement | # of improvement ideas per unit | 285 (avg /unit) | 300 per unit/yr 31 managers x300=9300 (775 month) | YTD total is 2974 YTD average 647 |

## ACT

**Act/Adjust**

Print Date / /

Figure 2. A3 Business Performance System (cont.)

173

| Hospital Operations VP Stat Sheet: | | Department: | | | | | Rev.9    01/28/13 |
|---|---|---|---|---|---|---|---|
| | | M | T | W | T | F | |
| Dates | | | | | | | **Notes** |
| **Daily Measures** | | | | | | | |
| **Safety** | | | | | | | Monday |
| Tell me about any Patients/Families at Risk | | | | | | | |
| Tell me about any OSHA recordables in the past 24 hours | | | | | | | |
| What quality issues surfaced in defect huddle? | | | | | | | |
| Tell me about the experience level of RNs on each of the next shifts | | | | | | | |
| **Quality** | | | | | | | |
| Discuss an Quality Opportunities or concerns Falls, bundles, chf, pneumonia, med rec/errors | | | | | | | |
| What are you learning from your rounding? | | | | | | | |
| What readmissions did you identify today? | | | | | | | |
| What processes are you monitoring today? | | | | | | | Tues |
| **People** | | | | | | | |
| What Problems/Barriers can I help remove? | | | | | | | |
| Who needs the most support today (weakest link) | | | | | | | |
| Tell me about any anticipated overtime or forceovers | | | | | | | |
| Tell me about any Physician or Leadership issues | | | | | | | Wed |
| What staff or provider can we recognize or celebrate today? | | | | | | | |
| **Delivery** | | | | | | | |
| Any areas where Demand exceeeds Capacity? | | | | | | | |
| How many patients? | | | | | | | Thurs |
| How many discharges/admits? | | | | | | | |
| How many admits did you receive in the past 24 hours? | | | | | | | |
| Have identified any avoidable days? | | | | | | | |
| What patient flow issues are you most concerned about today? | | | | | | | Friday |
| Any patients >5 days LOS; is there a discharge plan? | | | | | | | |
| What is your projected mesh variance? | | | | | | | |
| Does your team understand what is causing the variance? | | | | | | | |
| Do you have a plan to manage the variance and what is it? | | | | | | | |
| **Cost** | | | | | | | |
| Anything that will positively or negatively impact financials? | | | | | | | |
| What did you do differently today to move your productvity metric? | | | | | | | |
| What is today's priority - link to top metric? | | | | | | | **To Do's** |
| How can I help in prioritizing or removing barriers? | | | | | | | What Who When |
| **Friday** | | | | | | | |
| What trends are you seeing in the stat sheet data? | | | | | | | |
| What did we learn about the business this week? | | | | | | | |
| **Anything else to mention or Celebrate?** | | | | | | | |

Figure 3. Hospital Operations VP Stat Sheet

174

**VP Monthly Stat Sheet**     VP:     Month:

| Daily Measures | Week One | Week Two |
|---|---|---|
| **Safety** | | |
| Measure your teams' focus on employee safety | | |
| How often do you talk to them about it? | | |
| What EOC issues are you experiencing? | | |
| Do you know where your are vulnerable? | | |
| **Quality** | | |
| Are you aware of any readmissions today? Have you coached anyone on any process related to reducing readmissions / improving care transitions? | | |
| What SW is being observed? | | |
| If applicable: Are your root cause action plans on track? How are you developing others in this area? Learning? | | |
| Have you had any patient or customer or MD complaints today? | | |
| **People :** | | |
| What are your managers doing to develop their supervisor/leads? | | |
| What tools are they using? | | |
| How are your managers working their engagement plans? | | |
| **Delivery Flow** | | |
| How do you know SW for CC is being followed? | | |
| Have you observed any bottle necks in flow today? Response? | | |
| How are you coaching your managers on pace, expectation and level loading their work? | | |
| **Cost:** | | |
| Are you observing any successes or challenges in staffing to demand today? | | |
| Are you aware of any issues that are impacting net revenue? (e.g. denials, clin doc issues)? | | |
| Any celebrations re: removing waste? | | |
| **Concerns:** | | |
| Are your people performing? | | |

**Notes**

*Evidence of progress/action:*

| | Kamishibi | Safety | EOS | Waste Removal | Focus on pt |
|---|---|---|---|---|---|
| Lori | | | | | |
| Tara | | | | | |
| Mary | | | | | |
| Renee | | | | | |
| Donna | | | | | |
| Cindy | | | | | |
| Melanie | | | | | |
| Tom | | | | | |
| Kathy | | | | | |
| Bobbie | | | | | |
| Jodi | | | | | |
| Randy | | | | | |

**Follow-up & Notes**

Figure 4. VP Monthly Stat Sheet

## Daily Performance Huddle

| | |
|---|---|
| Trigger | **Scheduled/predetermined time for Huddle** |
| Done | **Huddle executed per standard** |
| Performed By | **Business Unit Leadership Team** |

Last Updated **10/18/13**
Rev. Number **7**
Revised By **D**

Owner **Patsy**
Takt Time

Work
In
Process

**Diagram, Work Flow, Picture, Time Grid**

Tip ◆ Tollgate ◉ WIP ▽ Critical Step ✚ Team Safety

**Daily Performance Huddle Board**

| | Major Steps | Details (if applicable) |
|---|---|---|
| 1 | Manager, supervisor, leads and staff gather at Daily Performance Huddle area/board. | |
| 2 | Start by reviewing "Work in Progress" (These are your just-do-Its and PDSAs.) *Briefly* review "Just Do Its". Any barriers to moving forward? | • Move completed work to "Improvement Ideas Implemented" section of the board. |
| 3 | *Briefly* review PDSAs. If the status indicator is green, acknowledge the work and move on. If the status indicator is red, ask about the barriers. | • Red and green status indicators should be used for PDSAs. ✓ If the work is on track (no new defects, adequate resources, no barriers to moving forward, etc.), owner should make sure status is indicated as green. ✓ If the work is not on track (new defect, resources needed, barriers to moving forward, etc.), the owner should change the status indicator to red and indicate why during huddle. Note: These red/green indicators represent daily status of the *work* on the PDSA and NOT the metric monthly or year-to-date roll-up. • Move completed work to Improvement Ideas Implemented" section of the board. |
| 4 | Review and record any **new** improvement opportunities identified. (Use Improvement Opportunity Form.) | • Question whether any opportunities were identified on stat sheet that day. • Ask staff what barriers they are encountering in their day. |

Figure 5. Daily Performance Huddle

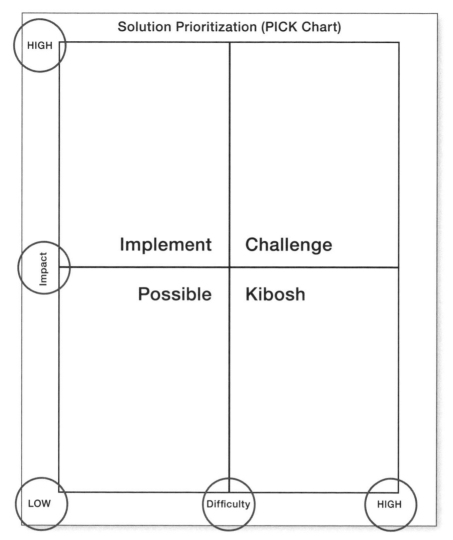

Figure 6. PICK Chart

# NEW IMPROVEMENT OPPORTUNITY

Name: _____ Date: _____

What is the problem? _____

_____

_____

What is happening? _____

_____

_____

Potential Solution: _____

_____

_____

True North Impact: (Circle one) Safety   Quality

Customer Satisfaction   People   Financial Satisfaction

Owner: _____

| Who | What | By When |
|---|---|---|
| | | |
| | | |
| | | |

Date Done: _____

Figure 7. New Improvement Opportunity form

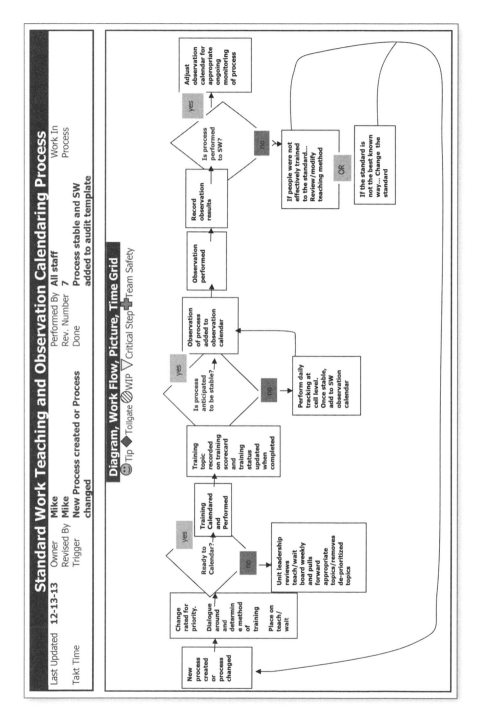

## Standard Work Teaching and Observation Calendaring Process

| Last Updated | 12-13-13 | Owner | Mike | Performed By | All staff | Work In |
| | | Revised By | Mike | Rev. Number | 7 | Process |
| Takt Time | | Trigger | New Process created or Process changed | Done | Process stable and SW added to audit template | |

### Diagram, Work Flow, Picture, Time Grid
☺ Tip ◆ Tollgate 🍥 WIP ▽ Critical Step ✚ Team Safety

**New process created or process changed** →

**Change rated for priority. Dialogue around and determine method of training** →

**Place on teach/wait**

**Unit leadership reviews teach/wait board weekly and pulls forward appropriate topics/removes de-prioritized topics**

**Ready to Calendar?** — yes → **Training Calendared and Performed** → **Training topic recorded on training scorecard and training status updated when completed** → **Is process anticipated to be stable?**

**Ready to Calendar?** — no

**Is process anticipated to be stable?** — yes → **Observation of process added to observation calendar** → **Observation performed** → **Record observation results** → **Is process performed to SW?**

**Is process anticipated to be stable?** — no → **Perform daily tracking at cell level. Once stable, add to SW observation calendar**

**Is process performed to SW?** — yes → **Adjust observation calendar for appropriate ongoing monitoring of process**

**Is process performed to SW?** — no → **If people were not effectively trained to the standard... Review/modify teaching method**

**OR**

**If the standard is not the best known way... Change the standard**

Figure 8. Kamishibia Board / Process Observation Standard Work

| Title: | Pharmacy Controlled Substance PDSA | Fresh Eyes: | |
|---|---|---|---|
| PDSA Owner: | Jordan | Team: | |
| PDSA Coach: | | | |

**Background/Current Conditions**

A FMEA was conducted due to a diversion that occurred at AMC. A need was recognized by the organization to develop and implement a daily method for controlled substance surveillance, due to the potential for diversion. Pharmacy recognized that the patient specific medication process for controlled substances had more opportunity for diversion than AcuDose pulls, or kit filling based on the number of handoffs and the lack of any closed loop tracking in the process. Pharmacy began to pareto the trends contributing to unresolved discrepancies in September 2012, putting more rigor into the process at AMC in December 2012. TCMC began gain consistency with their reconciliations beginning March of 2013. TCMC adjusted the pareto chart to gather stratified data in order to understand top contributors beginning in July 2013.

**Initial Problem Statement:**
Pharmacy has no method for controlled substance reconciliation which could result in patient and staff safety issues, failure to meet regulatory and legal compliance, and theft for each medication dispensed

What- Potential for Diversion
Where- AMC/TCMC
When- Daily
Who- Hospital Staff
How- There is no reconciliation process for controlled substance dispense from pharmacy
How Many- Every time the NarcStation is accessed
Consequence- Patient and Staff Safety, Regulatory and Legal Compliance, Theft

**Problem Statement**
From 1/1/13 to 3/30/13 AMC was able to reconcile 94.9% of controlled substance dispenses from pharmacy for specific inpatient dispenses, AcuDose closed loops, or NarcStation discrepancies daily. TCMC was able to reconcile 97.6% of controlled substance dispenses from pharmacy for specific inpatient dispenses, AcuDose closed loops, or NarcStation discrepancies daily. This results in a 96% reconciliation rate for AMC and TCMC combined. Failure to reconcile 100% of dispenses could result in patient and staff safety issues, failure to meet regulatory and legal compliance, and theft for each medication dispensed.

**Goals/Targets**
The goal is to Increase the percentage of reconciled partial dose controlled substance dispenses from 96% to 100%.

PLAN

| Coach Signature: | |
|---|---|

Figure 9. Pharmacy Controlled Substance PDSA

| Subject Experts: | Christi, Wendy, Dana | Start Date: | 01/30/2013 |
|---|---|---|---|
| | | Revision Date: | |
| | | Revision # | 1 |

**Analysis/Root Cause/Countermeasures (potential solutions)**

1. The January 2013 AMC pareto showed that 46.3%, or 19/41, of pharmacy discrepancies were caused by lack of documentation for all components of partial dose dispenses. The root cause of this was believed to be the lack of ability to pull partial doses from the automation due to the limitations of the software. In response, pharmacy began work on implementing a method for partial dose dispensing from NarcStation.

THEDA♥CARE                    Jan-13         Pharmacy Narcotic Reconciliation Pareto

2. In February 2013 lack of nursing documentation in Epic became the top contributor. There had been a recall of products supplied to us from Ameridose, leading to pharmacy compounding of Ativan and Midazolam drips. Premixed drips became available to pharmacy again mid-March, which decreased the discrepancies in pharmacy around lack of nursing documentation due to pharmacy compounding drips patient specific.

PLAN

Figure 9. Pharmacy Controlled Substance PDSA (cont.)

3. TC and AMC representatives met to discuss data stratification for TC pharmacy. It was determined that the pareto should be adjusted to better reflect the discrepancies seen at the TC campus. Data will be collected and analyzed through the month of July to determine top contributors and subsequent countermeasures.

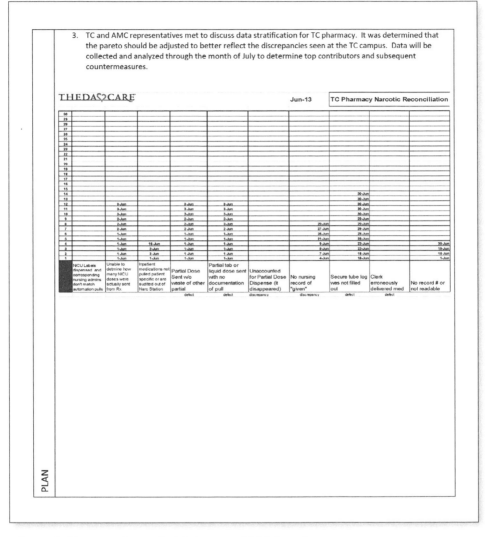

Figure 9. Pharmacy Controlled Substance PDSA (cont.)

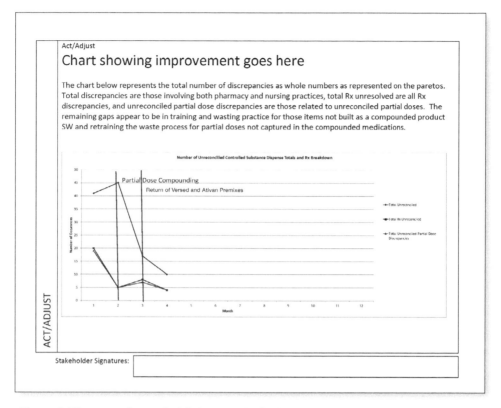

Figure 9. Pharmacy Controlled Substance PDSA (cont.)

| | Major Steps | Details (if applicable) | Time |
|---|---|---|---|
| 1 | Review Definitions of business unit and leadership team. | **Business Unit:** A defined piece of the business to which a manager is assigned operational responsibilities<br><br>**Leadership Team:** Comprised of individuals with operational responsibilities for performance results (i.e., manager, supervisor, lead,) and individuals who are responsible for support functions depending on need.<br><br>**Example support functions:** Education, IT, HR, OD, Finance, TIS, DR, Marketing, Quality, Purchasing, Facilities, Materials Management, Care Management, Physician Partners, other Unit Managers, Staffing Resources, Imaging, Environmental Services, Medication Safety Officer, Safety Officer, Biomed and other Operational Leadership. **Team members may be ad hoc or regular members** | PLAN |
| 2 | Identify everyone that supports your business by role and name. Group into Core Team members or "As Needed" members of your leadership team. | Of the Core Team Members select those roles you feel need to be represented each month to **OWN** the metrics that your team agrees on.<br><br>Using a SIPOC to identify customers, suppliers, inputs, outputs and process will help you with this identification. (See SIPOC standard work on TIS website) | PLAN |
| 3 | Assemble the Leadership Team monthly to review Scorecard Drivers and Watch Indicators. *(See Initial Meetings 1=3 and Monthly Performance Review Meeting Standard Work)* | Schedule the meeting after financial data is available (4th-6th business day) | DO |
| 4 | Evaluate the effectiveness of the team at the Monthly Performance Review Meeting | Do we have whom we need and do we need everyone we have? | STUDY |
| 5 | Make changes to team per evaluation and performance to metrics. Continue to operate as a single leadership team. | | ACT |

**Figure 10. Standard Work for Leadership Teams**

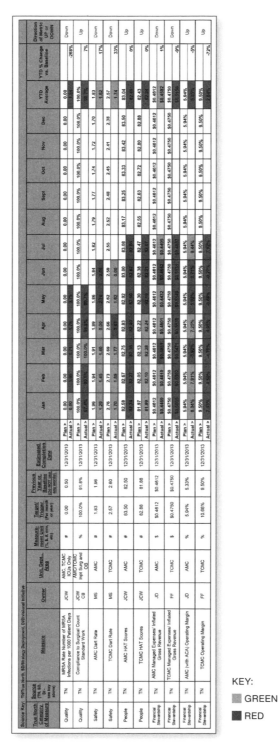

Figure 11. 2013 Monthly Review Scorecard

| Measure | Yes | No |
|---|---|---|
| **Performance** | | |
| • Is team achieving goal | | |
| • Are they improving | | |
| • Are they stable | | |
| **Visual Management** | | |
| • Can we see performance | | |
| • Can we see top contributor | | |
| • Action planning: fruitful? Evidence of Root Cause | | |
| **Huddle Board** | | |
| • Evidence of current and active problem solving | | |
| • Business rules clearly posted | | |
| **Standard Work** | | |
| • Standard Work observation active and visible | | |
| • Leader SW up to date and available | | |

**Gemba Summary** — Week: ___ VP: ___

Other Notes:

Figure 12. Gemba Summary

# Glossary

**A3:**  The A3 refers to the standard paper size on which a full problem-solving cycle is depicted for use by a team. The A3 includes a problem statement, business context, possible root causes, counter-measures, results of experiments, and next steps in sections labeled Plan, Do, Study, and Act. The standard form notes the project owner, time lines, and sponsors of the project.

**Countermeasures:**  An action or device deployed to correct a problem or to prevent a potential problem. An alternative term for "solution," which implies that the ultimate answer has been found and the issue does not need further review.

**Driver:**  At ThedaCare, a driver refers to a target or goal on a unit scorecard. "Reduce 30-day hospital readmissions by 50%" and "Eliminate surgical site infections" are both drivers that will lead the work of improvement teams. All drivers are intended to improve True North metrics.

**Gemba:**  A Japanese word popularized by the Toyota Production System, gemba means the place where real value is created for the customer. This is almost never in a boardroom or executive office. In a hospital, gemba is located wherever caregivers are directly helping patients because that is what is of value to the customer/patient.

**Hoshin kanri:**  A method for selecting the critical few initiatives on which to spend an organization's energy and then deploying that work. Developed in a few major Japanese companies during the quality movement of the 1950s, hoshin kanri helps leaders focus their strategy and keep major improvement projects on track.

**Huddle boards:** Large display boards—we use magnetic white-boards—for the display of improvement projects, new ideas, organizational metrics, performance over time, and reasons for celebration. This is the visual display of a team's work and is the focal point for daily meetings.

**Kaizen:** From the Japanese symbols meaning "change" and "good," kaizen is usually translated as "change for the better." In lean organizations, kaizen refers to projects and improvement events in which a cross-functional team studies and then improves an area or process in one week.

**Kamishibai:** Boards that help to organize audits of standard work. These boards usually have pockets for every day of the month which hold cards indicating what pieces of standard work, administrative or clinical, will be reviewed by leaders that day.

**PDSA:** Plan, do, study, act is the ongoing cycle of improvement as defined by W. Edwards Deming. This is another way of talking about the scientific method, in which we define problems, develop hypotheses, create experiments to test the hypothesis, analyze results, take action, and then begin again.

**Poke yoke:** Translated as "mistake proofing" in Japanese, this refers to methods or devices that prevent or correct errors at the point of creation. In a hospital, this might mean placing an operational button for an x-ray machine behind a lead curtain so the technician is forced to operate at a safe remove.

**Reverse fishbone:** A cause-and-effect diagram in which we begin with the desired outcome and then identify the actions that we believe will create the effect we seek.

**Scorecards:** A visual management tool that lists the targets for a unit, clinic, area, or division to achieve, all directly related to the organization's top-line metrics that guide our annual improvement projects.

**Sensei:** A teacher of great experience.

**Stat sheet:** Short for "status of the business," this is a daily conference between clinical lead and manager, and between manager and vice president, about incidents that have occurred and what issues might arise during the day.

**Standard work:** The written set of step-by-step instructions for completing a task using the best-known methods. Standard work is agreed upon by an improvement team and should be rewritten or changed only by another improvement team because a better way has been found.

**True North:** The few selected enterprise-wide goals that guide all improvement work. At ThedaCare, those goals or targets are selected annually and fall into five categories: safety, quality, people, customer service, and financial stewardship.

## References and Further Reading

James P. Womack, Daniel T. Jones, *Lean Thinking: Banish Waste and Create Wealth in Your Corporation*. New York City: Free Press, 2003.

John Toussaint, MD, Roger A. Gerard, *On the Mend: Revolutionizing Healthcare to Save Lives and Transform the Industry*. Cambridge, MA: Lean Enterprises Institute, 2010.

John Toussaint, MD, Arnold Milstein, S. Shortell, "How the Pioneer ACO Model Needs to Change: Lessons from Its Best-Performing ACO." *JAMA* (2013) 1341–1342.

Arun Shukla, "FAT Results from Lean Implementation: A National Process Approach to Lean Success." Princeton, NJ: Kepner-Tregoe, 2005. kepner-tregoe.com/PDFs/Articles/FAT_Results.pdf (last accessed July 29, 2011).

David Mann, *Creating a Lean Culture: Tools to Sustain Lean Conversions*. New York City: Productivity Press, 2005.

S. Spear, H. K. Bowen, "Decoding the DNA of the Toyota Production System." *Harvard Business Review* (September–October 1999) 96–106.

John Shook, *Managing to Learn: Using the A3 Management Process to Solve Problems, Gain Agreement, Mentor and Lead*. Cambridge, MA: Lean Enterprises Institute, 2008.

Masaaki Imai, *Gemba Kaizen*. New York City: McGraw-Hill, 1997.

C. Loyer, "The Fishbone Diagram and the Reserve Fishbone Diagram Concepts." March 16, 2009. processexcellencenetwork.com/articles (last accessed July 29, 2011).

Jeffrey K. Liker, *The Toyota Way: 14 Management Principles from the World's Greatest Manufacturer*. New York City: McGraw-Hill, 2004.

# Index

Page numbers in *italic* indicate figures. An *n* after a page number indicates a footnote.

## Endnote

This book was published by the ThedaCare Center for Healthcare Value. The Center was created in 2008 by the board of trustees of ThedaCare, a regional health system, with the intention of transforming the healthcare industry to provide better value for patients. The Center offers education in lean healthcare and assists organizations that are implementing lean thinking.

Using the experiences of ThedaCare and other high-performing healthcare organizations, the Center creates and is constantly expanding its curriculum of books, videos, experiential learning opportunities, and peer-to-peer collaborative learning networks. Many resources are free. This book is just one offering for organizations seeking to align leadership practices with lean thinking. For more information, visit createvalue.org.